Citizen Teachers and the Quest for a Democratic Society

Gerald K. Wood

Citizen Teachers and the Quest for a Democratic Society

Place-Making, Border Crossing, and the Possibilities for Community Organizing

Gerald K. Wood
Educational Leadership
Northern Arizona University
Flagstaff, AZ, USA

ISBN 978-3-031-15463-8   ISBN 978-3-031-15464-5 (eBook)
https://doi.org/10.1007/978-3-031-15464-5

© The Editor(s) (if applicable) and The Author(s), under exclusive license to Springer Nature Switzerland AG, part of Springer Nature 2022
This work is subject to copyright. All rights are solely and exclusively licensed by the Publisher, whether the whole or part of the material is concerned, specifically the rights of translation, reprinting, reuse of illustrations, recitation, broadcasting, reproduction on microfilms or in any other physical way, and transmission or information storage and retrieval, electronic adaptation, computer software, or by similar or dissimilar methodology now known or hereafter developed.
The use of general descriptive names, registered names, trademarks, service marks, etc. in this publication does not imply, even in the absence of a specific statement, that such names are exempt from the relevant protective laws and regulations and therefore free for general use.
The publisher, the authors, and the editors are safe to assume that the advice and information in this book are believed to be true and accurate at the date of publication. Neither the publisher nor the authors or the editors give a warranty, expressed or implied, with respect to the material contained herein or for any errors or omissions that may have been made. The publisher remains neutral with regard to jurisdictional claims in published maps and institutional affiliations.

Cover pattern © Melisa Hasan

This Palgrave Macmillan imprint is published by the registered company Springer Nature Switzerland AG.
The registered company address is: Gewerbestrasse 11, 6330 Cham, Switzerland

To Sebastian and Sophia and to their teachers who I hope will always inspire them to make the world a more just place.
To Christine who inspires me with the love for stories.

Foreword

One road a teacher can choose is to concentrate every day, with all your might, on justice. And one way to be a teacher of teachers is to think of that, and how to personify, to demonstrate, to talk, but to walk as well. Gerald Wood is that educator. He personifies, activates, and demonstrates to teacher candidates how he has chosen to act on a faith in justice which takes the profession, and the professional, from a platform of relative privilege out to the community, the school, the street not far from where he works. Read this book if you want to find your own way to bring energy and significance to the moral meaning of your life's work, education.

I have had a forty-five-year career in education and went from high school classroom teaching, to teaching the Social Foundations of our field in university in a way that has been driven by the demands of a nagging conscience, a sense that we all dine at a table set by giants *and* demons. The dream of a more fair, democratic, and just world demands something special of those who occupy the space of public education. For such a life can be *merely* lived feeding working-class children to the machine of late-capitalist political economy where profits are hoarded and political advantages secured, by the willful, cynical, neglect of the needs of school children. Teachers without a way to reflect on how their work could be, without care, implicated in this crime run the risk of losing the moral meaning of education, which John Dewey reminded us of was a spiritual, if still firmly secular, belief and action in our human responsibility to children, their "overall growth and development," working in every day *as if.* As if we might act on the imagination that every single child was treated by the school as the "best and wisest" parent might treat their own.

When he chose to work in my university college of education, I only knew that I could hope the way Gerald advocated then for Social Foundations teaching would come to pass. He started showing his commitment on day one, working with community and college activists on a Friday literacy project. And never stopped. Simply put, his is part of that bigger critical vision of teacher education where nobody, who carries a professoriate in a state-chartered College of Education, ever forgets for one minute that it is the life chances of children and citizens, in a democratic commonwealth, in our schools, which justify our existence. The work it takes to do this is professional education of the highest moral order, but it takes the work of not only teaching, but organizing, mentoring, community action, *four-dimensional* student engagement, and it takes working against the grain of university conformity, timidity, and performance. In short, doing this kind of work it is awfully tough to write, to tell, to share with the larger university audience, the work you have done. Here, to my great relief, Gerald Wood has done that service. For I worried for years that the complexity of his community and institutional organizing would never reach eyes of another diligent teacher educator, to inform, inspire, and build community across global platforms. But here it is, for you to take in, a local story, told by Gerald, but one you can relate to, connect with, and hopefully build your own connections through.

The reader might think twice about taking as a model the stories Gerald unfolds here. For Dewey's ideals, without a comprehensive understanding of what that commitment requires, degenerate to an idealistic bromide. The first thing it requires is a constant self-examination of personal history, and the moral arc of one's own life, as a way to sharpen the sense that this one teaching life be lived among those most nearly touched by obstacle after obstacle. And this living among is that demonstration for the professor, the teacher of teachers, to maximize their time in the community, attentive to the energy of social struggle present in each one. And only then to bring an accompaniment, building networks with the university where possible, and where it's not, waiting for the next opportunity, not giving up.

The demands of conscience and the *development* of Freire's conscientious justice also demand that the reader of this book ask students, with Gerald, "what keeps you up at night?" I respect the complexity and challenge of this question. But it first demands you ask yourself that question. For the working teacher, here is the problem, one of the things that keeps them up is the way state neglect, poverty, immiseration of work life brings children to them in underfunded, undersupported schools. And what keeps teachers up at night is also the demand of their own families, also suffering from worsening conditions. For the working teacher educator, falling to sleep without sharing the weight of the demands on the working teacher, the ones who fill our classes, and make our work possible .... well that kind of sleep is what it is, a luxury.

Gerald is wise here to include a key building material, the organizational power of teacher unions, both traditional and novel, as in the Red for Ed movement, and he honors the tradition of those teachers who built a house of labor, not just collegiate privilege. He would ask that new teachers find solidarity in organizing and see their profession for how it can put pressure through the political process, with the power of teacher unity. This can be a challenge, especially in university communities where there are few institutional rewards, and not a few punishments awaiting those faculty who organize as knowledge workers, and make justice demands both with and for their own students, and for their own professional working conditions.

Communities of color bear the reality that dreams of opportunity and justice for their children are fading under late-capitalist regimes, political power centers, not merely less democratic, but growing in a kind of existential hostility, where race hatred, white male dominance hierarchies, bleed out into the hallways of our public schools from the bodies of babies. It is a world where the very tissue of history is torn from the body of knowledge and teachers face the punishing, disciplinary surveillance of reactionary state school committees. Teachers in training face this world, and in the state, where Gerald Wood and I have taught, Arizona, it is in play in every school into which we might send a candidate teacher. Gerald writes of ways teachers can think of the *space* they occupy, school space, community space. For all these years I have seen what he has done not just to occupy this space in his own work, but to activate it, to insist that this be an active occupation, forming committees, organizing work groups, finding allies, and enabling students from educationally marginalized communities to re-claim these spaces for their own organizing.

And Gerald asks the reader to follow him to the community. For, he doesn't just tell, but show how taking that first step to find the families, the parents who are the children's "first teachers." And from there to know that organizing work, including those families can follow the ordinary, yet extraordinary trajectory where the public "intellectual" the professor in a university setting can move from mere traditional intellectualism to the organic intellectual demanded by any justice-based democracy. This is a critical democratic project to be sure and responds to critical needs and critical public responsibility, in critical, even emergency conditions. Gerald reminds us in this work how essential it is to face such organizing challenges by building relationships, friendships, and to do this work with optimism, a sense of inspiration and joy, wherever it can be found. And finally, this work when done with commitment and that spirit of love leads to a way that such challenging work can be, surprisingly, energizing and a kind of fulfillment of life's meaning, a teaching life against the alienation of professional isolation, a deepening curse in the modern university. This book is an example of a way to know yourself and learn to know the possibilities for democratic action and fulfillment. It is also a way to think, as a teacher, or teacher educator, building your own spaces for democratic life, to tell your own story, in your own community life. It will be busy and might involve coffee. Or chocolate. Enjoy.

Professor Emeritus, Social Foundations Guy Senese
of Education, Northern Arizona University
Flagstaff, AZ, USA

Preface

My life has always been about geography, often unrecognized, and about the crossing of borders. During my childhood, my family moved from place to place every couple of years—the United States, Mexico, Colombia, Ecuador, and Venezuela. My father's work in the banking industry prompted the majority of early childhood moves. These moves created a sense of not being rooted or belonging to any one place. I would not recognize until later that each of the places where I resided had significant unrecognized stories within the dominant contexts—the stories of Indigenous communities and their ancestral homelands, stories about the land and the fact that the naming of these lands was contested, and the resilience and resistance that undergirded the survival of and continual contestations from these Indigenous communities.

I was born in the suburbs of Middlesex, NJ; grew up in Caracas, Venezuela; went to boarding school in Lakeville, CT; attended college in Atlanta, GA, and Washington, DC; taught in Asuncion, Paraguay; and later completed my doctorate in Tuscaloosa, AL; and most recently am cultivating roots in Flagstaff, Arizona. As a Third Culture Kid (TCK) with a "United Statian" father and a Paraguayan mother raised in an upper-class family, I moved between "United Statian" and Latin American cultures while attending American Overseas Schools and growing up bilingual/bicultural at home.[1]

---

[1] I use the term United Statian to identify as someone born in the United States. In Latin America, the term American signifies anyone from the Americas. As my sixth-grade students in Paraguay asked me, "Where are you from?" I answered, "American" and they responded by saying, "So are we."

Each of these transitions required remaking and reshaping the spaces of schooling, home, work, as well as my own conceptions of self and belonging.

I first began my college career at Georgetown University studying political science, considering the Foreign Service, and envisioning a career in public international law. Inspired by a Jesuit focus on community service, I chose an internship at the end of my junior year where I spent the summer in southern Jersey traveling to different migrant farmworker camps translating for an attorney and a paralegal about the conditions in the labor camps and sharing "know your rights" information. Visiting these labor camps and seeing indentured servitude in the United States slowly eroded my belief that the United States was inherently better than the places where I had grown up. When farmworkers were forced to buy basic supplies from the overseer and ended up owing more than they made, there was no way out.

As a 21-year-old, my first introduction to the criminal justice system occurred when my boss told me a group of farmworkers had been macheted by their boss with the flat part of the blade and had gone into hiding. Armed with a camera, I went to find the workers, took pictures of the bruises, and drove the farmworkers to report the crime at the local police station. When I arrived, the police officer told me there was a warrant out for their arrest; this appeared to be based on some trumped-up charges made by the overseer, which the police officer appeared to believe. I showed the pictures of the bruises that had become less visible since the day of the beating. The officer said they did not have anyone who spoke Spanish who would be able to take their statements; I offered to translate what had happened as well as offer a written translation of what had happened. I found out many months later the overseer had moved to another state and started doing the same thing; there were no consequences.

When I returned to campus in the fall, I continued learning about the impacts on migrant children who had a discontinuous and broken schooling. Through a follow-up to the internship, I learned more about the U.S. involvement in the Salvadoran Civil War (1979–1992). The U.S. government denied political asylum to Salvadoran citizens in the 1980s who were fleeing the civil war generated in the midst of death squads that had killed 70,000 people. But in the early 1990s, the U.S. government allowed for a Temporary Protected Status (TPS) program to allow Salvadoran citizens to live and work in the United States for a period of time. As I look back on this more than 25 years later, I am still committed to immigrant rights issues. I see how deeply these experiences have been etched into my thinking around social justice, equity, and exclusion.

Through the Center for Social Justice Research (CSJR), Teaching, and Service at Georgetown, I was introduced to the ideas of providing access to educational opportunities to working-class Students of Color, which would spark a lifelong interest in education. I engaged in the Saturday Morning Program, where a group of college students picked up Black and Latine[2] children from one of the neighborhoods and explored the Smithsonian or played outside amidst the flowering cherry blossoms. Through the DC Schools Project, I tutored children of color in their homes once a week. This focus on promoting a commitment to education became more central and would lead me away from work in the foreign service.

In the early 1990s, the CSJR led me to work with an afterschool program and later become a preschool teacher at Georgetown Children's House, a preschool and an afterschool program, in the early 1990s. I vividly remember Melvin, a four-year-old Black boy, who in many ways was my first teacher. On the third floor of an old building in the Georgetown neighborhood, he would say in a deep voice, "Mr. Wood, you should tell us to line up before we go downstairs for lunch." Through his constant reminders about what children needed to be successful, Melvin was showing me deeper lessons that I was not ready to see. Melvin started to struggle, I let him sleep a little longer each day lowering my expectations without ever questioning my own biases. However, to be able to see these relationships across social class and racial identities more clearly, it was not sufficient to interact with children. In many ways, I entered teaching in the way many of my teacher education students do today—"I love children" and "I want to make a difference." I don't recall thinking or examining white privilege or having conversations that would have instilled the ability to cross cultural borders more fluidly and less naïvely.

I entered the field of education more formally when I moved back to Asuncion, Paraguay, in 1995 to be near family. Over the course of seven years, I taught first and sixth grades at St. Anne's School, a private,

---

[2] I use the terms Latine and Indigenous throughout the book unless I am referencing specific nationalities or tribal affiliations. While the term Latinx is being used instead of Latino/a to be gender inclusive, this term has not caught on in Latine communities; Latine is seen as more aligned with the Spanish language. I use the term Indigenous to acknowledge the global context of Indigeneity. At Transition School, Chicane parents started to bring out connections to Indigenous communities.

bilingual, Catholic school. In the mornings, I would teach all the subjects in English. In the afternoons, I was the high school International Baccalaureate (IB) Creativity, Action, and Service (CAS) program coordinator and special events coordinator. It was here that I started to question issues of privilege.

For one assignment with my sixth-grade students, I had them generate surveys on self-selected topics to understand bar graphs; I was confronted by the elementary school principal and told all the topics would have to be approved by parents. In particular, she singled out one topic—the impacts of the Stroessner dictatorship. Since these topics were chosen by students, I stood my ground. In these surveys, sixth-grade students wanted to identify perceptions and feelings about the Stroessner dictatorship. The implications of high school students who sat in the same classroom and whose parents had either been supporters of Stroessner or whose parents had been killed led me to think about the broader implications of the very present and violent histories that created chasms of difference. What were the consequences of the 35-year dictatorship of Alfredo Stroessner (1954–1989) on education? When adults entered the classroom, all the students in my class would stand up and say in unison, "Good morning, Mr. or Mrs. So and So." These demonstrations of authoritarianism and knowing how to challenge these demonstrations marked the ways in which knowing this school community was essential.

As the community service coordinator at the same school, I also sought to build relationships with the neighboring public school. The school wall had been knocked down, and I asked the school principal if we could partner with the school and build relationships as well as help build a wall. The principal looked at me and said, "Gerald, parents would never accept that we build relationships with those kids. You can help the school, but we are not building relationships." Divisions between working-class and upper-class families were highly enforced and manifested in daily interactions children and families had with maids, chauffeurs, and gardeners who worked in their homes.

These divisions in social class were also manifested in the pay and respect teachers received. My counterpart, Kitty Aquino, who taught Spanish to the same sixth-grade students, was an experienced educator who was pursuing her doctorate as well as teaching at the university at night. I questioned why Paraguayan teachers who taught the same subjects and often were much more experienced were paid less than the English-speaking teachers; most often Spanish-speaking teachers came from working-class backgrounds. On the other hand, English-speaking teachers often had no certification or experience. Within the context of a private school, I saw how social class, English, and whiteness were tied together.

As special events coordinator, I organized events to celebrate Halloween, Easter, or 4 July. Macarena, one of the high school students, asked me, "Hey Mr. Gerald, why don't you ever organize anything for Paraguayan Independence?" Caught, I blubbered something about not knowing enough about it, but I would be happy to organize if she would help. The celebration of Paraguayan Independence, Día del Folklore (Folklore Day), and a stronger commitment to honoring Paraguayan history and culture came about because of this one courageous question.

In the early 2000s, Paraguay was undergoing a transition to recognize Guarani as one of the two official languages in the country and working to promote bilingual education—Spanish and Guarani. While my mom was growing up in Paraguay, upper-class folks, particularly women, were discouraged from learning Guarani since this was an important social class marker that was deeply interwoven in whiteness and socio-economic status.

It would not be until I went to the University of Alabama in Tuscaloosa for my doctoral program that I would have language to ask these questions more intentionally. I would return to this question about bilingualism and the role of Guarani in Paraguay as a graduate student working with Dr. Tomlinson, who asked me to draft an article regarding language policy in Paraguay. In essays for Dr. Erevelles, I would analyze the questions that troubled me about my work with Indigenous communities realizing I did not have the language to adequately address the experiences I had encountered.

When I started a project with the Toba community in Paraguay, the students would gather food and clothes, and we would arrive in a chartered school bus. Seeing the families surround the bus, grab for the different bags, and often leading to fights, this felt viscerally wrong. I asked the vice-principal, Jacinta Monzón, who was fluent in Guarani if we could set up a community service project that did not include dropping clothes and other things out the bus windows. The vice-principal set up a meeting with the community to discuss the idea of growing some kind of collaboration, and we all gathered in a circle. Not speaking Guarani, I asked Jacinta, "What did they decide?" She replied, "Everyone has spoken." Naively, I asked, "So what did they decide?" The community spoke about the need for a shed to house their art, but in an I-know-better moment, this shed would first be a school garden and later a chicken coop. The school garden was short-lived because the responsibility fell on the principal. And the chicken coop did not account for the migration of community members outside of the Toba community to find jobs. These projects were bound to fail because they were not what the community needed or wanted. This failure came long before I understood the power of just listening. I remember driving back to my school with the four remaining, half-starved chickens in the trunk of my car. I gladly gave the chickens to one of the custodians.

For my dissertation, I mapped geographies of violence looking at how spaces and identities were constitutive and explored how schools were sites of violence—labeling and marking young people often creating spaces of exclusion in the public domain of schools. Documenting the ways in which identities were tied to places, I shared my findings with the principal of what I called Middleview Middle School. Disregarding this research, the administration moved quickly to create new categories of exclusion to privilege white, middle-class families who wanted the school to construct new categories of giftedness and advanced tracking to maintain segregated classes. I realized then that focusing solely on the school without examining and organizing the surrounding community would nullify any attempts to make change. It was time to move on.

So I came to Arizona with the hopes of working with and organizing the surrounding communities to consider how these relationships might shape the work in schools. In 2006, I accepted a position at Northern Arizona University (NAU) as a teacher educator in the Department of Education Leadership teaching Educational Foundations classes. I recognize the incredible privilege of a university and a teacher preparation program as a space that allows faculty to think about these issues while permitting me to evolve new sets of skills and language.

Teaching and researching for the last 15 years since coming to NAU in 2006 my questions have become more fully formed. These are some of the questions I hope to grapple with in this book.

- How do we check our own biases and consider how our own lived experiences impact what we do as educators?
- How do we begin to listen to communities that have been underserved and underheard?

- How can teachers in the United States contribute to advancing less partisan politics and broker the deep racial tensions in society?
- How can we, as citizen teachers, work to transform the political, cultural, and social landscape that would allow young people, their families, and their communities to have greater educational opportunities?

I include this journey because I invite you as teacher candidates, teachers, or educators to ask your own questions within the spaces you have created and identify your own journey as you envision your calling more.

Flagstaff, AZ, USA   Gerald K. Wood

Acknowledgments

This book was many years in the making and reflects so many relationships that have shaped my appreciation for community organizing. When I first moved to Flagstaff, AZ, I knew I wanted to work with communities, but I did not know that this path would connect me with community organizing through the Northern Arizona Interfaith Council (NAIC). I am indebted to Dr. Leah Mundell, Jason Lowry, and Roxana Deniz along with all the folks with whom we have organized to advocate for immigrant rights.

The development of Public Achievement (PA) at NAU would not have happened without Dr. Rom Coles and Dr. Miguel Vasquez. Becky White was a tireless advocate who modeled generosity, humility, and a deep knowledge of the families at the school. Jacob Dolence, Lauren Berutich, John Kester, and Noelle Johnson inspired me with their commitment to organizing and developing the structure for PA. I am also appreciative for Sierra, who I met in one of the First Year Seminars and inspired me to see where this work can take us.

I am thankful for the many parents, teachers, and students who were engaged in this work. The parents who shared their stories, their pain, and their hopes all channeled the dreams of so many families who understood their rights and sought to secure better futures for themselves and other families. I cannot express my appreciation to the many teachers who saw such potential and dedicated even longer hours away from their families to speak to a vision of how we could make the school more welcoming for all families.

I am reminded of the endless optimism along with the countless meetings to think of three students—Katie, Amy, and Amanda—who traveled with me to the Paulo Freire Freedom School in Tucson and would later create structure for a vision that we hoped would create new alternatives.

To the many students who have welcomed a commitment to justice into their lives and who have sought to recreate spaces anew to be more just, I am indebted to you for your fierce and tireless commitment. Working with colleagues Sarah Fix, Annie Watson, Michelle Novelli, and Jeff Lang has allowed me to embrace the possibilities of K-12 educators and union organizers committed to social justice.

The Marks family has constantly guided me to honor commitments to Indigenous peoples and Indigenous lands. I am forever grateful for the ways in which they have mentored my students and I to honor where we come from. With selfless commitment to educating those around them, Darrell and Makaius continue to plant seeds that will always be resilient and grow.

I am so appreciative for the people in my life who have honored stories and pushed me to tell these particular stories—my life partner, Christine Lemley, and our dear friend Laura Theimer, who is a storyteller in her own right. I am immensely appreciative of the close reading of the manuscript but also for accompanying me on these journeys. Christine has also taught me the power of this work when it is truly grounded in relationships.

I am forever grateful to have crossed paths with my mentor and friend, Dr. Guy Senese, who has always pushed me to acknowledge the struggle in the work and has pushed to me think about what justice looks like on the ground. His advocacy for the moral authority of educators and his modeling of thinking through the consequences of ideas and actions have shown me what it means to grapple with ideas with both humility and boundless curiosity.

Contents

1. **Citizen Teachers: Why Teachers Should Organize**   1
   - *Opening Vignette*   1
   - *Introduction*   2
   - *Teachers' Working Conditions*   4
   - *Divestment from Public Education*   6
   - *Community and Education Organizing in Chicago*   7
   - *#RedforEd*   10
   - *Conceptualizing Citizen Teachers*   12
   - *Situating Myself as a Citizen Teacher*   15
   - *Organization of the Book*   17
   - *References*   18

2. **Place-Making as Citizen Teachers: Analyzing Using Critical and Racialized Geographies**   21
   - *Opening Vignette*   21
   - *Introduction*   22
   - *Place-Making in Schools and Communities*   23
   - *Thinking Spatially*   26
   - *Mapping the School Context*   29
   - *Conclusion*   31
   - *References*   31

3 The Power of Teacher Organizing — 33
Opening Vignette — 33
Introduction — 34
Whiteness and White Spatial Imaginaries — 35
Border Crossings and Border Pedagogy — 37
Community Organizing Concept: Self-Interest — 38
Community Organizing Concept: Power — 39
Community Organizing Skill: Individual Meetings — 41
Context of Teacher Organizing — 43
Organizing for Mutual Accountability — 44
Lessons Learned — 50
Conclusion — 51
References — 51

4 The Power of Parent Organizing — 53
Opening Vignette — 53
Introduction — 55
Education Organizing — 55
Black Spatial Imaginaries — 56
Distinguishing Between Parent Involvement and Parent Engagement — 58
Community Organizing Concept: Public Accountability — 59
Community Organizing Skill: Conducting House Meetings — 60
Bridging and Bonding Spaces — 61
Stories from Parent Organizing — 62
Lessons Learned — 67
Conclusion — 68
References — 68

5 The Power of Student Organizing: Public Achievement — 71
Opening Vignette — 71
Introduction — 73
Public Achievement — 73
Community Organizing Concept: Public Work — 74
Community Organizing Concept: Everyday Politics — 75
Public Achievement in Action — 75
Lessons Learned — 80
Conclusion — 82
References — 83

6 The Power of Teacher Education	85
Opening Vignette	85
Introduction	86
Civic Engagement	87
1964 Mississippi Freedom Schools	89
Community Organizing Concept: Free Spaces	89
Student Involvement Days: Putting Freedom School Principles into Practice	90
Aspiring Educators Union Chapter: Social Justice Unionism	93
Lessons Learned	97
Conclusion	97
References	98
7 Conclusion	101
Opening Vignette	101
Introduction	102
Teacher Identities as Citizen Teachers	103
Border Crossings and the Mobilizations of Broader Collective Interests	103
Getting Started	104
Conclusion	105
References	106
Index	107

CHAPTER 1

Citizen Teachers: Why Teachers Should Organize

Abstract This chapter provides a historical and contemporary look at issues facing schools. After looking at some examples of activism and organizing, this chapter offers an initial conceptualization of citizen teachers. Citizen teachers work to direct the public's attention toward broader concerns in society while also working to alter relations of power in schools so educators can co-create more just schooling with parents, students, and communities.

Keywords Citizen teacher • Education organizing • Community organizing • #RedforEd • Democratic professionalism • Public work

OPENING VIGNETTE

As the neighborhood where the school was located experienced a wave of Immigration and Customs Enforcement (ICE) raids, we (my colleagues at a local charter school, students from my university classes, and I) considered how we could keep our students and families safe. We offered to drive children home to make sure they were not out on the streets and to make sure parents were home. In Arizona, ICE had detained 80 people, 16 in Flagstaff. While ICE claimed to have been pursuing folks with warrants out for their arrests or people who had violated their deportation orders, most of the people detained answered the door and could not show proof of their status (Hendricks, 2009).

© The Author(s), under exclusive license to Springer Nature Switzerland AG 2022
G. K. Wood, *Citizen Teachers and the Quest for a Democratic Society*, https://doi.org/10.1007/978-3-031-15464-5_1

I remember the morning in 2009 where I brought in a copy of the local newspaper talking about these raids. Maya, one of the middle school students, broke into uncontrollable sobs as she narrated that her stepfather had been deported. How could we as educators respond to this issue? How could we create conditions for students to engage in this issue that was so deeply personal and traumatizing while creating agency?

A year later, this young woman attended a protest against SB 1070—an Arizona law commonly referred to as "Show me your papers law." This law sought to criminalize undocumented folks and made it open season to racially profile Brown folks. Outspoken, engaged, and committed, Maya rode the bus with other elementary, middle, and high school students to attend the protest in Phoenix at the Arizona Capitol.

As she shared her experiences with me about high school the following year, her teachers saw her as disinterested and disengaged in class. One of her teachers threw out a challenge to give her the opportunity to present on a topic of interest. She came back to school the next day and told her teacher she was ready. In disbelief, the teacher allowed her to present. Maya spoke with tremendous passion and knowledge about the effects of SB 1070, knowledge she had gained firsthand in her immigrant rights work as well as her deeply lived experiences. With her social studies class speaking about the Holocaust, Maya connected the Holocaust with how Arizona was enacting immigration policies. These connections showed a young woman cognizant of the dangers of a law seeking to criminalize and profile people and the broader connections of the Holocaust.

Introduction

Dedicated, committed, and daring educators enter the profession with the hopes of making a positive difference in the lives of young people (Kozol, 1981/2009). Yet, a myriad of factors shape the experiences facing children and young people who enter public schools pushing educators to kindle the fires of this hope as they meet an ever increasing set of expectations. Public school educators also experience the effects of poverty, homelessness, segregation, the effects of immigration policies, and other inequities facing their students, families, and communities while trying to preserve their own livelihoods and avoid burnout (Anyon, 2014). As Maya's story highlights, school spaces can affirm the humanity of our students or reinforce how white supremacy is enacted through policies of exclusion.

With Immigrations and Customs Enforcement (ICE) raids in the community, the school staff where Maya went to middle school was attentive to the needs of undocumented youth and the impact these raids had on families. We made sure we understood as a school that schools were sanctuaries—law enforcement could not come in unless invited to do so. When our networks suggested raids were happening, we shared that information with families. Sitting down around the dinner table with students and their families to build relationships, share information, or connect family members to immigrant rights' work was critical to the relationships we developed in the school.

By intentionally situating the working conditions of teachers and highlighting the prime position in which teachers exist vis-à-vis working-class communities and Communities of Color, this chapter highlights the convergence of teachers' genuine self-interest and the "radical possibility" of engaging community organizing (Anyon, 2014). Anyon has so eloquently argued that educators are in a unique position to build movements with parents and students. Within these challenging contexts, teachers need to have the adequate tools to educate young people in their classrooms as well as actively function as engaged citizens in their schools, neighborhoods, and profession.

Citizen Teachers and the Quest for a Democratic Society: Place-Making, Border Crossing, and the Possibilities for Community Organizing explores how educators can expand our capacities to imagine what education can feel like when educators view ourselves as citizens first—as "place makers" who realize and act on our capacity to envision broader public spaces in the schools and communities in which we serve. We are also "border crossers" with the capacity to work fluidly and truthfully across cultural spaces (Giroux, 2005), and with this vision we are all also community organizers with the ability to identify and nurture the organic growth of young leaders in ways that make legible new relations of power. With this approach, families and communities, and in particular working-class Communities of Color, are visible co-creators in the remaking of these spaces.

Paying particular attention to community organizing work in one elementary school—Transition School—I weave stories and examples of organizing, specific tools and resources to support citizen teachers and educators in the work, and theoretical engagements to underscore the ways in which a deeply genuine praxis is possible. As someone who has experiences as a K-12 teacher, teacher educator, and organizer, I map out each of these engagements and connect those threads in ways that allow us as teachers to reconceptualize our own commitments. The stories of the achievements, the challenges, the failures, and the lessons learned all serve as touch points for educators carrying out this work. I raise the following questions for educators committed to a democratic society and democratic schools. What happens when educators join forces with parents and students to transform the learning conditions in schools? And what happens when educators enact their commitments as citizens first?

After speaking to teachers' working conditions and the ways in which the divestment from public education should be of concern to educators, this chapter maps out some of the broader issues impacting the educational landscape to consider the fight all public education educators need to consider if we are to generate a professional spirit and develop the intellectual and moral responsibility in our profession. After situating this work around the broader context of organizing in Chicago and Progressive Education, this chapter will define and conceptualize the role of citizen teachers.

Teachers' Working Conditions

> Now a professional spirit would mean not merely that the teachers would be devoted to the continuous study of the questions of teaching within the school room; but that they would also bear a responsibility as leaders, as directors in the formation of public opinion (Dewey, 1913, p. 38).

Most public school educators recognize the challenging working conditions and limited decision-making impacting teachers (Grumet, 2010). COVID-19, a global pandemic leading to school closures and new health protocols, has exacerbated the levels of stress experienced by teachers as educators grapple with concerns around health, technology, and trying to balance the needs of students and their own needs while bringing to light the limited control teachers have over their working conditions. Grumet has documented how this subordination of teachers has been effectively achieved through high-stakes testing, merit pay, scripted curriculum, and a host of other initiatives that have disempowered teachers.

As Dana Goldstein (2015) has pointed out, teaching has been an embattled profession which has been central to how we position teachers in the midst of a host of moral panics throughout our history in the United

States. The fueling of racialized fears at various times in our history, the embeddedness of white supremacy in the very fabric of our existence as a nation, and the criminalization of Black youth in schools have made visible the deeply embedded structures undergirding anti-Blackness.

But we have to ask what precipitates these moral panics in this day and age and what form do these attacks take? The attacks on teachers in the form of gag laws, bans on Critical Race Theory and books, and laws to out or censor LGBTQIA+ communities have made visible the fault lines that run beneath our classrooms making conversations about these issues even more necessary while making teachers' work more precarious. We continue to see politicians who attempt to control what teachers should do or not do. At least seven states (Arkansas, Iowa, Louisiana, Mississippi, Missouri, New Hampshire, Ohio, Oklahoma, Rhode Island, and West Virginia) have introduced or passed bills that prohibit the teaching of divisive issues such as race, sex, social justice, or Critical Race Theory (Schwartz, 2021).

While schools have arguably changed, the working conditions of teachers have not. Harkening back to the beginning of public education, attempts to control teachers are not new, particularly when we envisioned teaching as "women's work" (Apple, 1985). In 1904, Margaret Haley described low salaries, tenure concerns, large classroom sizes, and teacher workload. In the most telling aspect, Haley depicted the ways in which teachers were deeply embedded in an industrial model:

> And, lastly, lack of recognition of the teacher as an educator in the school system, due to the increased tendency toward 'factoryizing education,' making the teacher an automaton, a mere factory hand, whose duty it is to carry out mechanically and unquestioningly the ideas and orders of those clothed with the authority of position, and who may or may not know the needs of the children or how to minister to them (p. 389).

Dewey (1913) argued teachers lack professional spirit because they have so little control over the conditions of their work and are not given the "intellectual responsibility" over the curriculum and pedagogy. As we consider teachers' working conditions, we must identify ways in which educators' voices matter and support their efforts to stand as professionals with the autonomy and moral authority to speak to the issues of our time.

Divestment from Public Education

Public education is experiencing an unprecedented assault. The divestment from public education, the closure of public schools in working-class Communities of Color, and the privatization and chartering of schools highlight the entrenchment of white supremacy and the inner working of neoliberal capital to displace, marginalize, and exclude working-class Communities of Color (Lipman, 2011). In describing the neoliberal agenda, Gerson (2012) puts forth the following argument:

> So this has been not simply a question of the deregulation of the state's role. Rather, the state has stepped forward to enforce the profitability and privatization via *deregulation of things* (banks, corporations, charter schools) and the *elimination of regulations that protect people and basic rights* (labor, students, teachers, protestors, immigrants, etc.) while simultaneously *increasing punitive and disciplinary regulation of people* (Homeland Security, NCLB) (p. 100).

Corporate school reformers have sought to transform how we value public education by attacking public school teachers and teachers' unions and generating new forms of accountability that undermine public education (Karp, 2012). With legislation allowing charter schools in the 1990s, the proliferation of market-based reforms skyrocketed creating a new array of initiatives to defund public schools including creating school voucher programs, high-stakes testing, school accountability, and other tools to shut down "failing" schools and shift state monies to charter schools, religious schools, and private schools. In 2008, the economic collapse led by the housing market crash made possible the devastating cuts to public education as states grappled with lower tax revenues. As Leacham et al. (2017) highlight, state general funding per student still remains below the 2008 levels in 12 states as of 2017 (Oklahoma, Texas, Kentucky, Alabama, Arizona, West Virginia, Mississippi, Utah, Kansas, Michigan, North Carolina, and Idaho). Seven of these 12 states also cut income taxes (OK, AZ, MS, KS, MI, NC, and ID).

Corporate reformers have sought to eliminate unions and protections long fought for by teachers and teachers' unions. By positioning unions as obstacles to innovation and protectors of bad teachers, corporate reformers have worked to erode the power of unions to represent the needs of workers. Lipman (2011) has underscored how large cities in states with powerful unions have used charter schools as a way to circumvent these unions. In Wisconsin, Governor Scott Walker signed Act 10 into law eroding the power of collective bargaining of public unions by extending the time frame needed to call a strike (Schirmer, 2021).

COMMUNITY AND EDUCATION ORGANIZING IN CHICAGO

As I write this book and think about my own journey, I find myself pulled toward Chicago even as I live in Flagstaff. Chicago offers lessons for organizers. As a deeply divided American city, Chicago has been at the forefront of struggles around racial justice and labor organizing and this history serves as a catalogue of progressive causes. Jacob Riis' (2016) *How the Other Half Lives* and Upton Sinclair's (2019) *The Jungle* exposed the exploitation of labor and the living conditions facing immigrant communities.

Haymarket Square stands as beacon for workers around the world to honor May Day (Hagopian, 2021). The 1886 Haymarket Square rally to support workers for an eight-hour work day will be remembered for its legacy but also for the massacre that followed. The infamous trial of the Chicago Eight and the outright attack on anarchists and immigrants highlighted the deep divisions in Chicago. However, this city also gave rise to women labor organizers—Mother Jones (first a schoolteacher) and Lucy Parsons while also influencing folks like Emma Goldman—who understood the need to organize women and create alliances across diverse blocks. Drawing on David Harvey's (2008) analysis of class struggles over space, Don Mitchell (2008) argues:

> Thinking in these terms, it becomes easy to see a direct line from the protests at Haymarket Square on May 4, 1886, to the founding of the Industrial Workers of the World (IWW) in 1905. It is a direct line not only because some of the same people were involved, not only because Chicago in those years—as a space and place—was a crucible of radical formations from anarchists to socialist to feminists, but especially because both movements—the eight hours struggle of 1886 and the IWW in the first decades of the twentieth century—knew so well that in order to organize, in order to advance the class struggle, in order to make a world in a form appropriate to the needs and wants of working people control of *certain kinds* of places was crucial (p. 61).

Conversations about class struggle also gave rise to conversations about racial justice. With the formation of the Brotherhood of Sleeping Car Porters (BSCP), the Pullman Strikes by Black porters in 1894, led by Asa Philip Randolph and supported by Eugene Debs, highlighted the exclusion of Blacks from much of the labor organizing but also signaled the "rise of Protest Politics in Black America" (Bates, 2001). The attempts to maintain segregation between whites and Blacks in the midst of the Great Migration of Blacks out of the South starting in 1916 and the return of Black servicemen returning from World War I culminated in the 1919 Chicago Race Riots.

As Petra Munro has argued, "The period from 1890 to 1920 has been described as a period of female separatism, social activism, and belief in the special mission of educated women" (Gordon, 1990; cited in Munro, 1999, p. 19). Advocating for the right to vote, improved race relations, the participation of immigrant communities in community life, labor reform and the elimination of child labor, a growing peace movement among other issues, women invested considerable time and energy to recognize the importance of promoting democratic traditions. Munro (1999) has argued women fostered important community networks because they envisioned democracy as the result of these networks rather than individual rights.

Education Organizing

> Yet the history of Chicago teachers putting down their pencils and grabbing picket signs to defend public education dates back to the late nineteenth century—and contains some of the great stories in labor's history (Hagopian, 2021, p. 57).

In this context of this women's activism, the fight for better working conditions in schools was tied to the collective struggles for democracy. Among the earliest battles in Chicago where many of the women included here were, elementary school teachers were concerned about pension plans since they worked "in a system structured under the belief that teaching was a short-term job for a young woman until they married" (Rousmaniere, 2005, p. 36). In her early work as a union organizer, Margaret Haley fought for ensuring financial resources for school and teachers by tackling the corporations who were trying to evade taxes, thus linking education with broader corporate reform.

Paralleling conditions in schools today, Haley (1904) depicted the ways in which teachers were deeply embedded in an industrial model. This speech highlighted Haley's belief in the fundamental necessity of teachers to be involved in making decisions in the classroom foreshadowing the criticism of the role of administrators in the school hierarchy. In the same speech as the first woman to speak from the floor of the National Education Association and throughout her work with teachers' unions, Haley (1904) highlighted the connection between public schools and democracy.

> The essential thing is that public-school teachers recognize the fact that their struggle to maintain the efficiency of the schools through better conditions for themselves is a part of the same great struggle which the manual workers—often misunderstood and unaided—have been making for humanity thru their efforts to secure living conditions for themselves and their children; and that back of the unfavorable conditions of both is a common cause (p. 391).

With the lack of professionalism afforded to teachers, Haley pushed for teachers to see themselves as industrial workers to forge connections to the burgeoning labor movement.

Arguing teachers should take the power of their profession into their own hands because they will not be granted any special privileges, Counts (1932) believed teachers' power in schools is directly correlated to their power in society. As a matter of fact, as we continue to see today, teacher shortages have not led to an enhancement of teacher professionalism, teacher decision-making, or teacher pay. Apple (1985) has pointed to bureaucratization and rationalization of teachers' work through the imposition of hierarchies that remove decisionmakers and policymakers from the realities of teachers and classroom life. Counts (1932) believed teachers should be able to create connections across schools and communities to play a role "in the fashioning of those great common purposes which should bind the two together" (p. 28). Echoing Margaret Haley and John Dewey, the responsibility for schools should lie with the larger public, and teachers could serve as the nexus for this shared visioning. This visioning came together in 2018 with #RedforEd.

#REDFORED

#RedforEd became a rallying cry for educators often in Republican-controlled states armed in red shirts to signify a close connection to labor. Starting with educators in West Virginia on February 22, 2018, the call for a strike was unprecedented in right-to-work states with weak labor unions. What made this movement significant is the mobilization of grassroots activists who pushed the union leadership to adopt stronger actions. Of the 12 states which had not restored funding to 2008 levels and had also cut personal and/or corporate income taxes (Leacham et al., 2017), 3 of these (West Virginia, Oklahoma, and Arizona) led the #RedforEd statewide strikes/walkouts, and 2 states on this list (North Carolina and Kentucky) had one-day walkouts. This movement extended into democrat-controlled cities in 2019 such as Los Angeles and Chicago with work stoppages demanding better conditions for students and a broader movement around racial justice (Blanc, 2020). In showing the connections between Bargaining for the Common Good (BGC) actions and #RedforEd, McCartin et al. (2020) highlight important patterns in these diverse organizing centers:

> By taking to the streets, forming picket lines, striking, or marching on their state capitals, teachers demonstrated that there is no force more capable of freeing our schools from the strangling grip of austerity politics than organized teachers standing shoulder to shoulder with their allies... Whether they were mobilized behind carefully planned bargaining campaigns whose groundwork was laid over months or years, such as the Chicago teachers' strike of 2012 or the Los Angeles teachers' strike of 2019, or whether they took part in comparatively spontaneous insurgencies in settings where collective bargaining for teachers is not even allowed by law, such as Arizona where teachers struck in April 2018, teachers drew on the support of community allies and advanced untraditional demands (p. 99).

In these mobilizations, educators considered the broader implications for teachers as well as support staff in the schools. In West Virginia, educators chose not to end the strike until all state employees had received a 5% raise (McCartin et al., 2020). These strategic decisions to address a broader coalition worked in ways that industrial unions have not traditionally engaged. In fact, unions often followed unwillingly into discussing the call for strikes and in some states such as Oklahoma, the union called off the strike before educators were ready to go back to schools, sometimes losing important ground with demands as well as with their union members (Blanc, 2020). As Karvelis (2019), one of the co-founders of Arizona Educators United (AEU), suggested, "Arizona Educators United—a new organization, existing largely outside of established political power—was unable to be understood with the same logic that was applied to organized workers, social movements, or progressive politics in Arizona" (para. 5).

While Karvelis ultimately argues AEU was eventually institutionalized and subject to the same or even more extensive targeting as were its leaders, AEU highlighted the possibilities of creating movements outside of the established practices of social movements and existing political structures. This, in itself, is an important opening that allowed for new leaders who maybe did not see themselves reflected in their unions to implant new skills and new spaces. Dykes and Bates (2019) share, "Prior to her involvement with the AEU in the months leading up to the strike, Vanessa had never organized before. She had felt alienated from her union and thought that its priorities were especially disconnected from the everyday struggles of her bi- or multilingual students" (para. 28). Educators, many for the first time, saw the possibility to collectively organize and demand change.

Unlike Los Angeles and Chicago where organizers sought to secure "common goods" such as more school nurses or counselors and smaller class sizes (Blanc, 2020), the #RedforEd Movement failed to generate any specific demands around issues of race and racial justice. In addressing this invisibility of race in #RedforEd, McCartin et al. (2020) write, "Yet in other places, such as Tulsa and Oklahoma City, critical observer Lois Weiner found that the local unions failed to 'articulate demands that would speak directly to the aspirations and apprehensions of Black residents, parents, and students, who are educated in intensely segregated neighborhoods and schools'" (pp. 107–108). Karvelis (2019) highlighted how Arizona's burgeoning #RedforEd could not achieve this goal because many of the teacher-organizers did not think work around racial justice could occur in Arizona and often moved away from more contentious issues. Even though Arizona educators worked in solidarity with Indigenous educators through "Rez for Ed," the demands did not specifically engage the experiences of teachers and students of color.

While Kentucky only experienced a one-day strike across the state, Kentucky provides an important model for organizing as well as a more clear articulation of issues impacting Communities of Color. In contextualizing the work in Kentucky, Dyke and Muckian-Bates (2019) show how Black educators were already organizing "to prevent statewide takeovers, implement restorative justice programs, hire more Black educators, and create spaces within the union for Black educators to present concerns in a safe environment" (p. xy). With the rise of #RedforEd, Black educators were able to enlarge their demands around work that already had a foundation. As Kentucky shows, organizing around education cannot exist in isolation from other social movements for justice. By creating broad coalitions around an array of issues, educators stand a better chance of mobilizing communities and standing in solidarity with the children and young people they teach.

In identifying different forms of activism in the context of Chicago and #RedforEd, I identify these as important localizations for mobilization and see these as necessary conditions for fomenting new leadership. I also hope to make a case for why teachers should and may engage more in community organizing work rather than a protest politics.

Conceptualizing Citizen Teachers

In an increasingly partisan country where lively debate and discussions allow us to come together, these divides have generated less spaces of contact even within families, neighbors, and communities. As Hannah Arendt (1958/1998) states:

> To live together in the world means essentially that a world of things is between those who have it in common, as a table located between those who sit around it; the world, like every in-between, relates and separates men (sic) at the same time ... What make a mass society so difficult to bear is not the number of people involved, or at least not primarily, but the fact that the world between them has lost its power to gather them together, to relate and to separate them (pp. 52–53).

When we consider the context of schools, we have the ability to imagine a collaborative project around education. Dewey (1902) envisioned "schools as social centers" whereby schools could act as connecting spaces to regain the power to bring people together. Building on Jane Addams' formulation of settlement houses (Munro, 1999), Dewey drew on these collective experiences working with immigrant communities to generate solutions grounded in democratic practice. What vision has the ability to bring us together?

To bring people together across differences and mutual sites of convergence, this book is premised on the power of community organizing. In thinking through community organizing, Warren (2001) wrote:

> [R]elational organizing places relationship building at the heart of everything the IAF [Industrial Areas Foundation] does. This kind of organizing directly attempts to strengthen the social fabric and institutions of frayed communities, that is, to build bonding social capital. Relationships created across racial lines provide the foundation for bridging social capital (p. 34).

If our classrooms are to serve as spaces for social movement building and education is a fulcrum to create "radical possibilities" (Anyon, 2014), educators can foster the capacities to move more fluidly and fluently between schools and communities to generate more inclusive and powerful collective spaces to dream and imagine together. Community organizing allows us to build new capacities to alter existing power relationships. By identifying leaders who have the ability to bring people together, to articulate demands, and to change the existing power relations, community organizing relies on "people power" where communities may not have incredible financial or political power (McAllister & Catone, 2013).

What Is a Citizen Teacher?[1]

To conceptualize citizen teachers, I outline some key concepts to provide a theoretical frame through which to consider the relationship between education and democracy. Writing in 1932, Counts recognized the special role teachers have in representing "the common and abiding interests of the people" rather than reproducing the interests of the dominant class (p. 26). Following Counts' *Dare the School Build a New Social Order*, teachers should engage social issues of their times and nurture organic ties with communities.

---

[1] In thinking about the term "Citizen Teacher," I start with Rousmaniere's (2005) account of Margaret Haley by that name. This biography was my entry point into thinking about the central role women and particularly elementary school educators have played in addressing the working conditions facing women and the struggle for democracy at the turn of the nineteenth century. In addition, I credit Dennis Donovan and Harry Boyte, organizer/founder for the Public Achievement program out of Minneapolis, for guiding me to envision how community organizing can inform the work of citizen teachers.

John Dewey (2021) had faith and believed wholeheartedly in the collective intelligence of people when they could come together to identify problems and solutions. By bridging across divides of racial and ethnic backgrounds, social class, language, and other markers and sets of lived experiences, people's conceptions would be mediated by a range of experiences that would inform and enlarge our capacities to identify new possibilities. In critiquing the idea of detached professionals, an idea consonant with Progressive Education, Boyte (2008) argues the sense of professionalism instilled in professional programs has isolated professionals from the communities in which they work. While society had built up a cult of experts which had created some chasms of experience, Dewey believed we could broker new arrangements by cultivating new skills to broker these relationships across diverse lived experiences and values. Citizen teachers acquire the skills to cross multiple kinds of borders to acknowledge and work with communities.

Citizen Professionals

For Dzur (2018), democratic professionals have the ability to act as intermediaries between citizens and institutions, and thus expand democratic authority (pp. 13–14). Using their professional training, these professionals enhance their credibility through public collaborations where knowledge and authority are shared. In the context of schools, what does this mediation of families' interests look like within the context of shared decision-making, articulation of common goals around children's success, and the rebuilding of the public institution of schooling in ways that reflect the interests and needs of local communities?

Enacting democratic professionalism allows citizen teachers to picture a broader realm of authority grounded in their interactions with and understandings of the families they serve. Challenging the traditional view of politics as partisan, this alternative conception of politics locates the possibilities for re-energizing civic life in the productive possibilities of public work. "Public work is defined as the visible, sustained efforts of a diverse mix of people that produce goods—material or cultural—of lasting civic value" (Kari, 2007, p. 24). By focusing on public work, citizens (in the broadest sense of the word) are engaged in the process of the co-creation of the traditions, practices, and processes involved in sustaining the commons. Drawing on the concept of public work, citizen professionals bring together a broad array of skills to "rebuild the civic lives of communities in addition to their traditional role in providing specialized services to individuals" (*The Citizen Professional Idea*, n.d.).

The University of Minnesota Citizen Professionals outlines three main areas to demarcate citizen professionals: (1) identity, (2) body of knowledge, and (3) set of skills. "Citizen professionalism is mainly an **identity**: seeing oneself first as a citizen with special expertise working alongside other citizens with their own special expertise in order to solve community problems that require everyone's effort." For teachers who often struggle to identify resources one family at a time, what might this look like to help young people ask about hunger, homelessness, or unemployment? "Citizen professionals have a **body of knowledge** about the connections between the personal and the public dimensions of their professional practice." For teachers, what would it mean to foster a "sociological imagination" discerning the relationship between personal troubles (they have to do with his self and with those limited areas of social life of which he is directly and personally aware) and public issues ("a public matter; some value cherished by publics is felt to be threatened") (Mills, 2000, p. 8)? "Citizen professionals have a **set of skills** for facilitating public conversations and catalyzing public action. In the context of their regular service delivery, they are able to skillfully interweave the personal and public dimensions of the issues they and their patients or clients face. And when the time is ripe, they are able to bring together other citizens for public conversations and sometimes for small, local action projects to address community needs" (*The Citizen Professional Idea*, n.d.).

What might it look like to engage teachers and educators as community organizers? How might we nurture more humanizing spaces to understand the aspirations, hopes, dreams, and fears of the parents who put their children in our care? How can we identify leaders in their schools and communities to build networks of solidarity and translate these into power? How can we work alongside other community members who are working to address issues in local communities and underscore the bridging of these issues and the work educators do with young people in schools?

Situating Myself as a Citizen Teacher

As I describe in the Preface, my experiences moving between the United States and Latin America and my work in K-12 schools situated me in between curricular and extracurricular contexts recognizing the necessity and significance of mediating these distinct identities and spaces. Without addressing the privileged positions and moving outside of the realm of my own material and ideological positionings as an upper-class, bilingual, white, and Latino man, I would not be able to decouple the relationships among and between whiteness, English, and social class.

I started generating questions about the personal and the political aspects of my identity and the lived realities I encountered in Paraguay and New Jersey. Additionally, I began to recognize the injustices as I tried to engage communities—particularly working-class and Indigenous communities in Paraguay—through trial and error. Only with the privileged space to reflect on these experiences in graduate school would I be able to think more critically about my own identity and complicity in reproducing spaces of domination while developing a sociological imagination (Mills, 2000).

I started volunteering at the Mountain English Spanish Academy (M.E.S.A.)—a small charter school in Flagstaff. Through my different roles at the school—volunteer, substitute teacher, youth organizer, and governing board member, I sought to find ways to literally and figuratively cross borders to create organic ties to the community. This would entail starting to comprehend the impact of immigration policies on undocumented youth, the lack of infrastructure and investment in Communities of Color, and the absence of educational opportunities. The creation of afterschool programs from arts programs to Student Involvement Days (see more in Chap. 6) initiated my attempts to alter spaces to hear the experiences of youth while also attempting to create new educational opportunities. Each of these afterschool activities mapped out community strengths and issues in ways that were intended to apply the lessons from the 1964 Freedom Schools to lived realities in Flagstaff.

While I had a vision of what these connections between school and community could be, I did not have the tools to make these connections explicit. As a bilingual English-Spanish speaker with some exposure to immigration advocacy, I intentionally connected with different groups working to advocate for immigrant rights. Through word of mouth and meeting organizers, I started working with Northern Arizona Interfaith Council (NAIC). NAIC is an Industrial Areas Foundations (IAF) affiliate that would lead me to learn about community organizing. Attending a five-day IAF training introduced me to the ideas of Saul Alinsky and Ed Chambers; it allowed me to start visioning new ways of facilitating public actions and building collective power.

In 2009, several colleagues and I involved in community organizing work started developing some partnerships with both Community School and Transition School (pseudonyms) to bring in Public Achievement (PA) to the schools (see more about PA in Chap. 5). PA provided an important formulation of what classrooms could look like when organized around the idea of public work and when classrooms could serve as "movement-building spaces" (Anyon, 2014). It also served as a catalyst to think about my own teaching at the university and how this could further more community-engaged work. From 2011 to 2013, I would engage in community organizing work with Transition School to build off the work we had started through PA.

Along with PA, I had been participating in the school community as a translator for many of the Spanish-speaking families. I also encouraged the school to ensure families had access to adequate translation through the district. Additionally, I helped organize English classes for the families by coordinating with colleagues in the Spanish Department. These skill sets were significant in seeing how to mediate my own identity as a teacher with a broader conception of how to serve as an intermediary between the university and the communities we served.

After stepping back from the work with Transition School, I was pushed to consider how we can conduct community organizing work with others when we have not been able to successfully do this in our own spaces. In 2013, I started to consider how this organizing work could be enacted in my own college and how the creation of public work could facilitate the rendering of new spaces and social relations that challenged the status quo. All these spaces afforded me ways and words to reflect and act on educational policies and protocols in order to propose transformations to promote equity and justice; some of these goals materialized, many did not.

ORGANIZATION OF THE BOOK

In this chapter, I made a case for why teachers should organize and how we might conceptualize citizen teachers. By defining community organizing and contextualizing this work in one school, this chapter will move from broad national movements to the more localized ways in which teachers may effectively engage families and communities.

In Chap. 2, I outline how citizen teachers can recognize their role in place-making drawing on the field of critical and racialized geographies. I also provide ways to think about what a spatial analysis might entail and how this analysis may broaden the conceptions of citizen teachers.

Chapter 3 will introduce the role of teachers in organizing since this is the focal point as we regard teachers as border crossers. As I outline how teachers can engage in organizing, I problematize how whiteness and the broader context of white supremacy may prevent teachers from fully articulating a vision for schools and communities while offering practical resources to allow teachers to begin this journey.

In Chap. 4, I will turn toward parents as leaders in community organizing while showcasing how parents actively articulated visions for the school. While these efforts were tempered by administrators and teachers, these examples provide insights in to how schools that want to invite family engagement may structure their schools in ways that allow for parent leadership to thrive.

Turning to students and the work teachers can do in their classrooms, Chap. 5 will offer ways in which young people can engage in the construction of a public vision through Public Achievement. This chapter will also point to the limits of this work when not fully integrated into the work of teachers.

In Chap. 6, I consider how teacher candidates can start building up some of the skills needed to become citizen teachers. As colleges of education tend to be too narrowly constructed around teaching of discrete skills, how can we create and envision more democratic spaces?

References

Anyon, J. (2014). *Radical possibilities: Public policy, urban education, and a new social movement* (2nd ed.). Routledge.

Apple, M. (1985). Teaching and women's work: A comparative and historical analysis. *Teachers College Record, 86*(3), 455–473.

Arendt, H. (1958/1998). *The human condition* (2nd ed.). The University of Chicago Press.

Bates, B. T. (2001). *Pullman porters and the rise of protest politics in Black America, 1925–1945*. The University of North Carolina Press.

Blanc, E. (2020, October). The Red for Ed Movement, two years in. *New Labor Forum, 29*(3). https://newlaborforum.cuny.edu/2020/10/03/the-red-for-ed-movement-two-years-in/#

Boyte, H. C. (2008). *The citizen solution: How you can make a difference*. Minnesota Historical Society Press.

Counts, G. S. (1932). *Dare the schools build a new social order?* Pref by W. J. Urban. Southern Illinois University Press.

Dewey, J. (2021). Creative democracy—The task before us. In E. T. Weber (Ed.), *America's public philosopher* (pp. 59–66). Columbia University Press.

Dewey, J. (1913). Professional spirit among teachers. In D. J. Simpson, & S. F. Stack, Jr. (Eds.), 2010 *Teachers, leaders, and schools: Essays by John Dewey* (pp. 37–40). Southern Illinois University Press.

Dewey, J. (1902). The school as social center. *The Kettering Review* (2011), 29(1), 8–13.

Dykes, E., & Muckian-Bates, B. (2019). Educators striking for a better world: The significance of social movement and solidarity unionisms. *Berkeley Review of Education,* 9(1). https://doi.org/10.5070/B89146423. https://escholarship.org/uc/item/7zk5p5sw

Dzur, A. W. (2018). *Rebuilding public institutions together: Professionals and citizens in a participatory democracy.* Cornell Selects.

Gerson, J. (2012). The neoliberal agenda and the response of teachers unions. In W. H. Watkins (Ed.), *The assault on public education: Confronting the politics of corporate school reform* (pp. 97–124). Teachers College Press.

Giroux, H. A. (2005). *Border crossings: Cultural workers and the politics of education* (2nd ed.). Routledge.

Goldstein, D. (2015). *The teacher wars: A history of America's most embattled profession.* Routledge.

Gordon, L. (1990). *Gender and higher education in the progressive era.* Yale University Press.

Grumet, M. R. (2010). The public expression of citizen teachers. *Journal of Teacher Education,* 61(1–2), 66–76.

Hagopian, J. (2021). A people's history of the Chicago Teachers Union. In M. Charney, J. Hagopian, & B. Peterson (Eds.), *Teacher unions and social justice: Organizing for the schools and communities we deserve* (pp. 57–66). A Rethinking Schools Publication.

Haley, M. (1904). Why teachers should organize. In A. J. Milson, C. Haeussler Bohan, P. L. Glanzer, & J. W. Null (Eds.). (2004), *Readings in American educational thought: From Puritanism to Progressivism* (pp. 387–392). Information Age Publishing.

Harvey, D. (2008, September–October). The right to the city. *New Left Review,* 53, 23–40.

Hendricks, L. (2009, February 3). ACLU requests records of ICE raid in Flagstaff. *Arizona Daily Sun.* Retrieved May 6, 2012, from https://azdailysun.com/news/aclu-requests-records-of-ice-raid-in-flagstaff/article_009a1aed-fdd7-50c3-b849-ee554ef09855.html

Kari, N. (2007). Public work: A practical theory. In N. Kari & N. Skelton (Eds.), *Voices of hope: The story of the Jane Addams School for Democracy* (pp. 24–38). Charles F. Kettering Foundation.

Karp, S. (2012, Spring). *Challenging corporate ed reform*. Rethinking Schools. Retrieved from March 20, 2014, from http://www.rethinkingschools.org/archive/26_03/26_03_karp.shtml

Karvelis, N. (2019). Towards a theory of teacher agency: Conceptualizing the political positions and possibilities of teacher movements. *Berkeley Review of Education, 9*(1). https://doi.org/10.5070/B89146418

Kozol, J. (1981/2009). *On being a teacher*. Oneworld.

Leacham, M., Masteron, K., & Figueroa, E. (2017). *A punishing decade for school funding*. Center on Budget Policy and Priorities. Retrieved August 4, 2021, from https://www.cbpp.org/seven-of-twelve-states-with-deepest-k-12-cuts-also-cut-income-taxes

Lipman, P. (2011). *The new political economy of urban education*. Routledge.

McAllister, S., & Catone, K. C. (2013). Real parent power: Relational organizing for sustainable school reform. *National Civic Review, 102*(1).

McCartin, J. A., Sneiderman, M., & Weeks, M. B. (2020). Combustible convergence: Bargaining for the common good and the #RedforEd uprisings of 2018. *Labor Studies Journal, 45*(1), 97–113.

Mills, C. W. (2000). *The sociological imagination* (40th Anniversary ed.). Oxford University Press.

Mitchell, D. (2008). Which side are you on? From Haymarket to now. *ACME: An International Journal for Critical Geographies, 7*(1), 59–68. https://acmejournal.org/index.php/acme/article/view/810

Munro, P. (1999). Political activism as teaching: Jane Addams and Ida B. Wells. In M. S. Crocco, P. Munro, & K. Weiler (Eds.), *Pedagogies of resistance: Women educator activists, 1880-1960* (pp. 18–45). Teachers College Press.

Riis, J. (2016). *How the other half lives: Studies among the tenements of New York*. Benediction Classics.

Rousmaniere, K. (2005). *Citizen teacher: The life and leadership of Margaret Haley*. State University of New York Press.

Schirmer, E. (2021). The Wisconsin uprising – 2011. In M. Charney, J. Hagopian, & B. Peterson (Eds.), *Teachers unions and social justice: Organizing for the schools and communities we deserve* (pp. 77–80). A Rethinking Schools Publication.

Sinclair, U. (2019). *The Jungle*. CreateSpace Independent Publishing Platform.

Schwartz, S. (2021, May 18). Map: Where Critical Race Theory is under attack. *Education Week*. Retrieved June 13, 2022, from https://www.edweek.org/policy-politics/map-where-critical-race-theory-is-under-attack/2021/06

The Citizen Professional Idea. (n.d.). University of Minnesota. Retrieved August 5, 2021, from https://innovation.umn.edu/citizen-professional-center/the-citizen-professional-idea/

Warren, M. (2001). *Dry bones rattling: Community building to revitalize American democracy*. Princeton University Press.

CHAPTER 2

Place-Making as Citizen Teachers: Analyzing Using Critical and Racialized Geographies

Abstract This chapter considers how educators can and should pay attention to the spatial implications of issues impacting educators and schools. Drawing attention to critical and racialized geographies, this chapter provides examples of how we might think spatially and expand our roles as citizen teachers. If we are to alter relations of power and engage in place-making, we need to have the analytic tools to understand how community issues percolate into schools. This chapter introduces the school and the district to map out particular relationships that shape the narration of these stories and examples.

Keywords Critical geographies • Racialized geographies • Settler colonialism • Place-making • White supremacy

OPENING VIGNETTE

In 2017 in Northern Arizona, the Indigenous Circle of Flagstaff (ICF) was convened by Indigenous community members to address the possibility of recognizing Indigenous People's Day. A Flagstaff City Council member had presented this idea, but Indigenous communities expressed concern about the substantive nature of this day without meaningful participation and input from Indigenous community members. Through various community forums, the ICF gathered information and presented

© The Author(s), under exclusive license to Springer Nature Switzerland AG 2022
G. K. Wood, *Citizen Teachers and the Quest for a Democratic Society*, https://doi.org/10.1007/978-3-031-15464-5_2

a list of demands to City Council. During the forum on education, over 100 Indigenous youth mostly in attendance from one of the high schools identified the need for the inclusion of conversations impacting Indigenous communities.

In an effort to address this work more locally, my life partner, Christine Lemley, reached out to a high school in Flagstaff where many of the Indigenous students expressed a need to make connections to Indigenous issues as part of the curriculum. Drawing on the Kia Eke Panuku (Building on Success) model perfected over 20 years in Aotearoa, New Zealand, and in collaboration with Māori scholar, the school team implemented a Culturally Responsive Pedagogy of Relations (CRPR) framework (Bishop et al., 2010). These efforts were integrated by the Native American academic advisor (who was also part of the ICF) to make visible the lived experiences of Indigenous students.

During a workshop to engage staff around this CRPR framework, we highlighted the transformation of the physical space in the school. Before we started this work, most visuals included the school logo and articles/trophies highlighting athletics. With permission to engage differently, students approached the Native American academic advisor to create murals in the school. These murals began to legitimate the presence of Indigenous student more intentionally than before. As one of the teachers in the workshop said, "This is the difference between renting and owning." The permanence of the murals created a new set of relationships mapped on to the school building. While this by itself does not change the school culture, it mobilized a new set of relationships and questions.

Introduction

Public school teachers stand at the crossroads of powerful social and spatial forces shaping society. At the heart of these forces is the question of who has a right to make and remake public spaces or as Henri Lefebvre (1996) has said, "Who has a right to the city?" In this book, I argue these forces are about claims to who has a right to occupy, exist, and (re)make particular places. As Harvey (2008) has claimed:

> The question of what kind of city we want cannot be divorced from that of what kind of social ties, relationship to nature, lifestyles, technologies and aesthetic values we desire. The right to the city is far more than the indi-

vidual liberty to access urban resources: it is a right to change ourselves by changing the city. It is, moreover, a common rather than an individual right since this transformation inevitably depends upon the exercise of a collective power to reshape the processes of urbanization. The freedom to make and remake our cities and ourselves is, I want to argue, one of the most precious yet most neglected of our human rights. (p. 23)

Paraphrasing Harvey, the question of what kind of schools we want cannot be separated out from the kind of social relationships we envision and how we might collectively secure that vision for our schools.

In this chapter, I map out the ways in which critical and racialized geographies shape our discussions of spaces in schools. After theorizing these constructs, I offer the reader the opportunity to think spatially by applying these ideas to several different examples to uncover the spatial dimensions and to allow educators the opportunity to show how space matters. In order to situate the school where many of these stories unfold, I provide the context of the school to underscore how these particular stories were mediated.

Place-Making in Schools and Communities

Teachers are responsible for making and remaking spaces daily. Whether teachers organize their classrooms to invite inclusive and welcoming communities, create the conditions for children to value democratic principles, or work to dismantle white supremacy, teachers are responsible for the production of material, ideological, and pedagogical spaces in classrooms, hallways, playgrounds, or cafeterias. Schools, however, are rarely democratic spaces and often reproduce white supremacy through the ways in which policies and practices create school hierarchies (e.g. tracking and criminalization of youth) (Wood, 2006). If schools are responsible for the maintenance of white supremacy, how can teachers take a more active stance in dismantling this? How can relations of power be altered to make school leaders and teachers accountable to Communities of Color in the school? What tools may be available for teachers who recognize the need to challenge these processes and renew our focus on reconstructing public spaces and democratic engagements?

Production of Space

To draw on new ways of remaking space, I situate this work within the field of critical geographies (Lefebvre, 1994; McDowell, 1999). In Lefebvre's formulation, we often think of space as the backdrop on which things happen or view space as an empty space to be filled. However, as Lefebvre and other critical geographers contend, space is produced and fluid through the constituting of specific sets of relationships, ideologies, and practices (Lefebvre, 1994). Linda McDowell (1999) stated, "Places are made through power relations which construct the rules which define boundaries. These boundaries are both social and spatial—they define who belongs to a place and who may be excluded, as well as the location or site of experience" (p. 4).

When I worked on my dissertation in Tuscaloosa, Alabama, I was interested in interpreting how spaces were tied to particular identities and how specific spaces were produced through particular configurations of power (Wood, 2006). For example, the middle school had created a classroom for students who had faced disciplinary issues. Students in this classroom were not allowed to ride the bus, wore uniforms, and entered through one of the side doors after the other students had already gone to class. The classroom windows were completely covered so no one could see in and students could not see out. The classroom had its own bathroom and students often ate lunch after other students had finished or ate in their classroom to make the isolation complete. However, within these spaces, the teachers had connections to the students—whether as familial connections or connections that were generated from really coming to figure out students' stories—because of the shared isolation they faced. Even though the school tried to isolate these students, what kind of social relationships existed and what spaces were produced (Wood, 2006)?

When we see spaces as relational and consider the multiple points at which we might enter, we may wonder how individual neighborhoods are constituted and perceived and how this may shape the ways in which children and young people are read in the context of schooling. For example, we often ask teachers who work in schools to educate children from the neighborhood in which children reside, but we do not require or ask teachers to consider the histories, experiences, or lived realities of the residents in these neighborhoods. What might it mean for teachers who express fear to live in the neighborhoods where they teach? What might it mean for teachers to live in or be a part of the communities in which they teach?

Critical and Racialized Geographies

Before underscoring the production of racialized geographies, we must recognize that public schools and the many educators and families who attend these schools are on occupied lands still central to Indigenous peoples.[1] As uninvited guests, we recognize ancestral lands are critical to the stories and lived experiences of Indigenous peoples. The occupation of land has been rendered invisible the Indigenous communities that lay claim to their ancestral lands and sacred sites. How do we come to understand and produce spaces that acknowledge the sacredness of the land while recognizing our own complicity as educators in disrupting these relationships to the land?

How do we come to understand that production of spaces are always historically constituted and racialized? As Lipsitz (2011) has argued, "Racialized space has come to be seen as natural in this nation. Spatial control, displacement, dispossession, and exclusion have been linked to racial subordination and exploitation in decisive ways" (p. 52). Black and racialized geographies (Gilmore, 2002; McKittrick, 2011; Woods, 2002) provide us with both a language and set of lived experiences that allow us to understand how the production of space is never neutral.

School spaces are deeply entrenched in white supremacy. Jenkins (2021) has shown the ways in which anti-Black spatial imaginaries have determined Black bodies to be undesirable and therefore subject to exclusion. Demonstrating the ways in which Black folks have been terrorized in the United States, Jenkins parallels how schools are "sites of spatialized terror" whereby Black students live in fear—fear of violence, fear of removal, fear of discipline, fear of being subject to watching the exclusion of Black minds and bodies through the daily rituals and routinized mechanisms that are in place (p. 119).

Racial and Spatial Reorganization and Public Schools

Scholars have drawn attention to the racialized reorganizations of space in both New Orleans (Buras, 2014) and Chicago (Lipman, 2011). Both cities have experienced the overhaul of their public education systems in ways

---

[1] While I cannot do justice to the importance of this conversation around tribal identities, I cannot address critical geographies without emphasizing the impact of settler colonialism. In describing settler colonialism, Tuck and Yang (2012) speak to the disruption of ways of life, extraction of resources for profit, and ongoing reassertion of this daily violence.

that have intentionally displaced and rendered invisible Communities of Color while destroying the fabric of these communities. By repurposing many of these "failing" public schools into charter schools, these experiments in neoliberal accountability have been grounded in the gentrification of urban spaces to supply white and middle-class folks with new spaces to support the exploitation of Folks of Color. New Orleans experienced the devastating effects of Hurricane Katrina as a way to recreate the "failing" public school system into an array of charter schools leaving many of the most vulnerable children in vastly underfunded public schools. In suggesting the rebuilding of New Orleans after Hurricane Katrina re-established white control over the city's public school system, Buras (2011) argues:

> These reforms are a form of *accumulation by dispossession*, which David Harvey (2006) defines as a process in which assets previously belonging to one group are put in circulation as capital for another group. In New Orleans, this has included the appropriation and commodification of black children, black schools, and black communities for white exploitation and profit (pp. 303–304).

Both cities have used "failing public schools" as the mantra for this spatial reorganization through the recreation of an extensive network of charter schools.

Under the Renaissance 2010 plan to make Chicago the center of global capital, Chicago has closed hundreds of "failing" schools to remove Folks of Color from the city center. In responding to the attempts to close Dyett High School in a historically Black district in Chicago, Jitu Brown has highlighted these connections of school closures, privatization, and the broader context of anti-Blackness. Nguyen et al. (2017) wrote, "For Brown (2015), the destruction of public education connects not only cities across the United States, but also the social processes through which communities are colonized. That is, Brown (2015) highlights the centrality of education reforms in the production of racialized urban geographies" (p. 3).

Thinking Spatially

A premise of this book is that teachers think spatially but must expand the ways in which we as citizens make and remake spaces. If citizen teachers are to broaden the scope of their engagements and serve as cultural brokers between schools and communities, they must be able to analyze both how spaces are historically produced and how they can be recreated in ways that are more democratic. In seeking to address this spatial turn, critical geographers have paid particular attention to how education and schools are actively constituted as sites of both reproduction and resistance (McCreary et al., 2013). Critical geographers of education have often identified the ways in which power, place, and the formation of particular identities are deeply interwoven (Helfenbein & Taylor, 2009; Wood, 2006). Below I illustrate some examples—COVID-19 and mass school shootings—that would help educators start to think spatially while paying attention to multiple scales—national, state, or local. In addition, we also have to consider the differential impacts on Communities of Color when we consider the ways in which "the racialization of space and spatialization of race take place" (Lipsitz, 2007). As Lipsitz suggests, the relegation of communities to different physical spaces contributes to experiences of inclusion or exclusion.

COVID-19

In 2022, with more than six million deaths worldwide and over a million deaths in the United States alone, this global pandemic has been devastating in terms of loss of life. In addition, massive unemployment, closures of small businesses, impacts on working women, and the differential access to education have shown the social and spatial impacts of a pandemic (McPhearson et al., 2021). Grounded in specific policies and practices that have tried to create segregated spaces (Lipsitz, 2007), lack of access to affordable and high-quality housing, crowded conditions, lack of access to reliable transportation, and lack of access to adequate health care have contributed to severely impacting the well-being of these communities and making these "hotspots" for transmission (*Introduction to COVID-19 Racial and Ethnic Health Disparities*, 2020).

The COVID-19 pandemic has surfaced and made visible the vast inequities in schooling along the axes of race, social class, (dis)ability, and language, among other aspects. The uneven impacts of the COVID-19 pandemic on working-class Communities of Color in the United States show how the racialization of place has impacted Black, Indigenous, and Latine communities unevenly in the area of educational access and outcomes. The turn to online, remote learning has brought to light the massive disparities in access to technology and the ability of families to stay home with their children. Citizen teachers might listen to communities' needs and advocate for a range of possible solutions to ensure young people whose learning opportunities are most impacted would have access to in-person learning.

Mass School Shootings

Mass school shootings have garnered national attention and have produced new spaces and technologies for surveillance. After Columbine, schools had already shifted to transforming the architecture of schools in ways that make schools less accessible to intruders and families (Devine, 1997). The militarization of schools with more visible armed School Resource Officers (SROs), surveillance cameras, and the ability to seal off parts of the school building is a massive industry that has generated high profits for companies, but it has also contributed to how we structure spaces to make schools less accessible.

While Chicago and other large cities continue to face untold tragedies of young People of Color shot on their way to and from school, the visibility of school shootings in small town, suburban America requires a spatial analysis. In locating these school shootings in towns or suburbs with usually less than 50,000 people, what social relations exist and are produced? How does the fact that these shooters have mostly been white males contribute to a conception of the spaces that have been created in spaces that are often considered safe (Gammell et al., 2021)? With the shooting in Parkland, FL, in 2018 and the nationwide media attention generated by young folks from Marjory Stoneman Douglass High School through the subsequent activation of the March for Our Lives, the ideological and material production of space is central to this debate. More recently, another shooting in an elementary school in Uvalde, TX, has once again raised the specter of gun violence. Citizen teachers might wade into the debates about whether teachers should be armed and listen to the parents of the children whose lives were lost.

Mapping the School Context

Built in 1956, Transition School[2] bordered the university campus and in many ways existed on the margins of the school district. The school had also been the site of multiple conversations around potential closing and rebuilding since the city had expressed interest in creating a wider corridor along the main road that went past the school, which would have eliminated safe access to the school. In some ways, Transition School also was on the margins of the district because of the population it served—working-class whites, Latine, and Indigenous communities, as well as a small percentage of Black students and international families.

When I first visited the Transition School, I was struck by the language on the marquis—"You can't learn if you are not here." The same language was reflected in green and white banners throughout the school. The school had expressed concern about its 100-day Average Daily Membership (ADM) count, the way Arizona allocates funding for the following school year. With many families not enrolling or starting school right away, the school was concerned about potential funding issues. I share more about this messaging on the marquis and the school banners in Chap. 3.

The school had been rezoned when the district closed two of the smaller elementary schools in 2010, and the school now drew on families that lived further out. For the principal, the changing demographics and the longer commutes for many of the families had a detrimental effect on the school's achievement and parent engagement. This rezoning had compounded concerns around attendance and pass rates on standardized state tests. The principal highlighted how challenging this was for hosting any community nights and parent-teacher conferences. Some families now lived more than 30 minutes away and had to travel on the highway if they had access to transportation. The school was trying to figure out how to invite families to the school or even more importantly began identifying key locations in each community where the school officials could meet families.

Many of our early conversations between the principal and I centered on how to engage families within the context of their own neighborhoods. We identified specific sites in each neighborhood where families might go

---

[2] I term the school Transition School as a pseudonym because of its constant state of flux. The possibilities of expanding the road and the displacement of the school, the rezoning of school boundaries, and the shift to a magnet school all suggested the school's future was in flux.

and considered how we could host meetings with parents in a tavern, a library, or other landmarks in the neighborhood. In identifying places in the different neighborhoods, I was hoping we could recognize that for many families schools were not actually accessible while also acknowledging the fact that many Indigenous families had probably experienced historical or intergenerational trauma[3] through their own experiences with forced assimilation in military boarding schools. By having the school meet families on their turf, this would be a powerful way to invite families into a conversation and start breaking away from a unidirectional model of parent involvement. While extending these conversations, I was hoping to move the school in the direction of becoming a Community School, something that was not inherently part of the school's messaging.

Success for All

The school had also been using a Success for All Model (*Success for All*, n.d.). This model was brought to the school by two teachers who had attended a conference and convinced the principal to implement it schoolwide. Since I had expressed skepticism about the scripted nature of this program, the principal encouraged me to visit classrooms and decide for myself. During these walks, I found amazing teachers who used Success for All with ease and purpose, but I also saw teachers who struggled and had less experience and less mastery of teaching. I also observed one of the teachers who was involved in organizing sing praises of the program and then choose not to use it the following year because it was not working for some of her students. During the process of organizing, the school had only implemented the model at a K-2 level, but the school principal was pushing the grades 3–5 teachers to also adopt the model. This led to some tension where some of the teachers in the upper grades were not excited about the model; the principal told teachers who were not on board that they could leave. While I appreciated that this innovation was teacher led at the K-2 grades, the line in the sand the principal drew without input or

---

[3] Sotero (2006) has described historical trauma as the "psychological and emotional consequences of the trauma experience are transmitted to subsequent generations through physiological, environmental and social pathways resulting in an intergenerational cycle of trauma response" (p. 95). These intergenerational traumas can result from "colonialism, slavery, war, [or] genocide" (p. 93). In the school, Indigenous families had seen the results of the kidnapping and removal of children from their families and communities, forced assimilation, the loss of language and culture, and the violence exhibited in schools.

discussion seemed unnecessarily harsh and undemocratic. The school was in the process of implementing all elements of the model. This included the Solutions Teams—Attendance, Interventions, Parent and Family Involvement, Community Connections, and Cooperative Culture.

Conclusion

To engage as citizen teachers, educators must be positioned to discern the physical, cultural, and power-laden geography and landscape of their schools and communities. This requires expanding how teachers think about the organization of their classrooms to engage in a broader conversation about how we structure social relationships in the school and community. By drawing attention to specific national and statewide issues and underscoring the way these issues impact diverse communities, citizen teachers can start applying these augmented conceptions to their school communities. If we are to alter the way we envision relationships between parents and teachers, we must also recognize how spaces have been historically produced and have tools to remake these spaces.

References

Bishop, R., O'Sullivan, D., & Berryman, M. (2010). *Scaling up educational reform: Addressing the politics of disparity*. NZCER Press.

Buras, K. L. (2011). Race, charter schools, and conscious capitalism: On the spatial politics of whiteness as property (and the unconscionable assault on Black New Orleans). *Harvard Educational Review, 81*(2), 296–330.

Buras, K. (2014). *Charter schools, race, and urban space: Where the grassroots meets grassroots resistance*. Routledge.

Devine, J. (1997). *Maximum security: The culture of violence in inner-city schools*. University of Chicago Press.

Gammell, S. P., Connell, N. M., & Huskey, M. G. (2021). A descriptive analysis of the characteristics of school shootings across five decades. *American Journal of Criminal Justice*, 1–18.

Gilmore, R. W. (2002). Fatal couplings of power and difference: Notes on racism and geography. *The Professional Geographer, 54*(1), 15–24.

Harvey, D. (2008, September–October). The right to the city. *New Left Review, 53*, 23–40.

Helfenbein, R. J., & Hill Taylor, L. (2009). Critical geographies of/in education: Introduction. *Educational Studies, 45*, 236–239.

Introduction to COVID-19 Racial and Ethnic Health Disparities. (2020, December 10). Centers for Disease and Control Prevention. Retrieved June 6, 2021, from https://www.cdc.gov/coronavirus/2019-ncov/community/health-equity/racial-ethnic-disparities/index.html

Jenkins, D. A. (2021). Unspoken grammar of place: Anti-Blackness as a spatial imaginary. *Journal of School Leadership, 31*(2). https://doi.org/10.1177/105268462199768

Lefebvre, H. (1996). *Writing on cities* (E. Kofman & E. Lebas, Trans. and Ed.). Wiley-Blackwell.

Lefebvre, H. (1994). *The production of space* (D. Nicholson-Smith, Trans.). Wiley-Blackwell.

Lipman, P. (2011). *The new political economy of urban education.* Routledge.

Lipsitz, G. (2011). *How racism takes place.* Temple University Press.

Lipsitz, G. (2007). The racialization of space and the spatialization of race: Theorizing the hidden architecture of landscape. *Landscape Journal, 26*(1), 10–23.

McCreary, T., Basu, R., & Godlewska, A. (2013). Critical geographies of education: Introduction to the special issue. *The Canadian Geographer, 57*(3), 255–259.

McDowell, L. (1999). *Gender, identity and place: Understanding feminist geographies.* University of Minnesota Press.

McKittrick, K. (2011). On plantations, prisons, and a black sense of place. *Social & Cultural Geography, 12*(8), 947–963.

McPhearson, T., Grabowski, Z., Herreros-Cantis, P., Mustafa, A., Ortiz, L., Kennedy, C., Tomateo, C., Lopez, B., Olivotto, V., & Vantu, A. (2021). Pandemic injustice: Spatial and social distributions of COVID-19 in the US Epicenter. *Journal of Extreme Events, 7*(4). https://doi.org/10.1142/S234573762150007X

Nguyen, N., Cohen, D., & Huff, A. (2017). Catching the bus: A call for critical geographies of education. *Geography Compass, 11*(8). https://doi.org/10.1111/gec3.12323

Sotero, M. M. (2006). A conceptual model of historical trauma: Implications for public health practice and research. *Journal of Health Disparities Research and Practice, 1*(1), 93–108.

Success for All. (n.d.). Success for All Foundation. Retrieved January 10, 2022, from https://www.successforall.org/our-apprach-schoolwide-programs/

Tuck, E., & Yang, K. W. (2012). Decolonization is not a metaphor. *Decolonization: Indigeneity, Education & Society, 1*(1), 1–40.

Wood, G. K. (2006). *Mapping geographies of violence: Disciplining space and negotiating identity in middle school.* ProQuest Dissertations Publishing.

Woods, C. (2002). Life after death. *The Professional Geographer, 54*(1), 62–66.

CHAPTER 3

The Power of Teacher Organizing

Abstract This chapter highlights the work organizing with teachers at Transition School. In particular, this chapter highlights an organizing victory and the process for getting a bus for families. I contextualize how we set up the trainings for teachers and delve into a discussion of self-interest and power. I underscore the ways whiteness and white spatial imaginaries may hinder the work of teachers and how border pedagogies may allow teachers to start to work through their own limits of their lived experiences.

Keywords Teacher organizing • Border crossing • Whiteness and white spatial imaginary • Power • Self-interest • Individual meetings

OPENING VIGNETTE

The teachers and parents invited the district's Assistant Superintendent of Operations to visit the school. The group had decided to pursue this strategy because they were trying to request that the district provide a school bus for the families living in family housing on the university campus. In our meetings, the principal and several teachers expressed that many times the children living in family housing were late to school. In addition, the principal had expressed concern about the fact that many of the families in family housing would enroll and start school several weeks after the school year had started because these families did not return until the university started; this impacted enrollment numbers and funding for the school based on the 40-day count used for calculating staffing for the next year.

The parents expressed important concerns about safety—their children slipping on the icy hill in the winter, their children crossing the street on their own on a university campus, or their children often having to stand up on the university bus with college students and not be heard or helped. And the school had experienced young children trying to get home on their own either to family housing or to the affordable housing near the school. One story that stood out most was a first grader who never made it home after he left the school. He usually walked home alone to the housing development, and this particular day, he had been chased by a dog and got lost as he tried to run away. He was found bawling, afraid, and alone two hours later when the parents notified the school he had never made it home.

The district had hemmed and hawed about the bus. First, district officials expressed that the district could only provide transportation through federal funds if housing was located at least a mile away from the school. After the group had measured the distance and found the housing was exactly a mile away if measured to the top of the hill, the district said it could not get a large bus up the hill because there was not enough space to turn the bus around.

The teachers and parents believed the assistant superintendent would be able to see the challenges the families faced if he could walk the route. These students, often first and second graders walking on their own, had to walk down a steep hill and cross the street where they would wait for a campus bus. From there, the children would ride on the bus with university students to the stop that would allow them to again cross the street and walk through the fence to get to school. After walking the route with the families and the teachers, the assistant superintendent pushed to get a bus to address the morning route; this would allow the children to arrive on time and give parents some breathing room to make sure their children could get to school safely.

Introduction

For teachers and parents, this example of organizing showed the possibility of actually finding a common ground that would address their mutual concerns. In order to do this, however, we had to create the space for teachers and parents to articulate these needs in ways that highlighted the convergence of these interests by building deeper relationships grounded in values, stories, and lived experiences that allowed for the emergence of trust. We also had to strengthen the capacity of teachers and parents to be able to demand these changes by learning to see themselves as power brokers while learning how educational institutions worked; to make decisions; and to carry out strategies that had been polished from researching the multiple contexts, policymakers, and possible actions. In order to enrich these partnerships, teachers needed to build trust and relationships with families through a deep engagement in the issues impacting these communities, have a knowledge of the communities they are serving, and ensure accountability across these different spaces of school and home.

As I map out in this chapter, the work to actualize these relationships of both trust and accountability required underscoring the deep-seated beliefs and practices that framed the context of schooling for teachers. After discussing whiteness and white spatial imaginaries, this chapter addresses community organizing concepts—self-interest and power—and then describes the organizing context of the work with teachers.

WHITENESS AND WHITE SPATIAL IMAGINARIES

When I first started organizing with the school, the marquis read, "You can't learn if you're not here." When I first saw this message, I was puzzled. As a teacher educator and former early childhood, elementary, and middle school teacher, we generally recognize parents' guardians and families as a child's first teachers. This message was intended to address the importance of attendance in school every day. In conversations with the principal, attendance and the implications for funding seemed to be a central focus for her. However, the message on the marquis and the banners sent the wrong message about how the school envisioned a partnership and how they perceived families. After discussing this message with teachers and after several months of pushing on this message, the principal put up a new message, "Success starts here."

These messages about learning and success negated the important roles families and communities play in the nurturing and growth of children. What does learning mean? Are the things that children learning at home either irrelevant at best or miseducative at worst? What does success mean? Do schools have to erase/eradicate what children have learned in their homes or communities in order to be successful? How were these particular messages reflective of the demographics the school served—working-class white, Latine, and Indigenous students and in smaller numbers international families? What did educators believe about the families they served?

To apprehend the context of organizing in this particular school, we must examine whiteness and the racial practices in the school. In an interview, Michael Eric Dyson identifies whiteness as an identity, an ideology, and an institution (cited in Castagno, 2008, p. 319; Chennault, 1998). As an identity, representation of Folks of Color matters. Demographics of staff included predominantly white staff, two Navajo teachers, and no staff who were fluent in Spanish. The school hosted a person from Parenting Arizona, an organization to create family liaisons to support the needs of families. This person was of Navajo descent and was fluent in Spanish; she was often called into the office to translate for parents. In conversations with the principal about the need for more bilingual speakers (both Navajo and Spanish), the principal said she had to prioritize teachers with a special education background.

For Dyson, whiteness as an ideology refers to the "systematic reproduction of conceptions of whiteness as domination" (Chennault, 1998, p. 300). As an example, when I translated for Spanish-speaking parents in a classroom with an Indigenous educator, a parent asked if Spanish could be interfering with their child's progress. The teacher responded by suggesting the parent should really emphasize English at home. If English is the dominant language and whiteness is tied to speaking English, then ideologically the teacher is reproducing the dominance of English while devaluing the need for other languages. How does the normalization of English and its relation to whiteness get affirmed every day?

To reinscribe and reproduce whiteness, we have to consider the ways in which particular social relations of dominance imbue these spaces with meanings about what is appropriate and expected in particular locations. As we connect to the institutional ways in which whiteness is reproduced, the messaging on the marquis highlights the distancing that exists between families and the school. These markers all suggest a particular idealized parents that are embedded in white, middle-class norms. In describing the white spatial imaginary, Lipsitz (2011) writes:

> The white spatial imaginary idealizes 'pure' and homogenous spaces, controlled environments, and predictable patterns of design and behavior. It seeks to hide social problems rather than solve them. The white spatial imaginary promotes the quest for individual escape rather than encouraging

democratic deliberations about the social problems and contradictory social relations that affect us all (p. 29).

Rather than engaging in deliberation about learning, the school sent clear messages about expectations. Rather than looking to solve the problem, the school administration seemed more focused on pushing the multitude of reasons why children were absent under the rug while blaming families and communities. The significance of hiring more teachers with special education backgrounds rather than specific linguistic and cultural backgrounds suggests these foci are mutually incompatible. This was not an opening to a dialogue and eliminates the possibilities for collectively problem-solving.

While I pay attention to one school here, my experiences working with a small charter school and K-12 administrators in a doctoral program would suggest patterns of homogeneity when we consider how school leaders may focus on school climate and address parental involvement. As Schutz (2011) has argued:

> Public spaces, Dewey understood, are strangled by conformity. Unless people are willing to honestly reveal their individual perspectives, these spaces necessarily collapse. Instead of distinctive contributions, one will only get more of the same from each participant. Inequities of power, widely divergent interests, and other forces that might reduce the collaborative spirit of participants, then, must be kept to a minimum (p. 496).

If we are to envision schools as humanizing and affirming spaces, we have to find ways to destabilize our perceptions of what schools are intended to be. How can we listen to the needs of students, parents, families, and communities in ways that uphold commitments to nurturing democratic spaces?

Border Crossings and Border Pedagogy

Teachers, and educators more broadly, have to magnify their capacities to be cultural brokers—to manifest the ways in which culture plays out in classrooms, schools, and communities and to find ways to bridge these diverse experiences in ways that acknowledge community cultural wealth— "the accumulated assets and resources in the histories and lives of Communities of Color" (Yosso, 2005, p. 77). Grumet (2010) has argued educators often have limited exposure to working with families and other stakeholders. Teacher preparation programs generally focus more on preparing teachers for the classroom so practicums and student teaching placements tend to center teaching. How can teachers recognize the different forms of capital that families bring—the ability of students to translate for their families, the willingness of families to make sure their children are able to receive more education than they have had, the elaboration of skills that allow children to navigate culturally hostile spaces. In their classrooms, teachers bring together consciously or unconsciously students from different walks of life with different lived experiences and different knowledge bases. Giroux (2005) writes:

> Border pedagogy provides opportunities for teachers to deepen their own understanding of the discourse of various others in order to effect a more dialectical self-critical understanding of the limits, partiality, and particularity of their own politics, values, and pedagogy. By being able to listen critically to the voices of their students, teachers also become border-crossers through their ability to make different narratives available to themselves and to legitimate difference as a basic condition for understanding the limits of one's own knowledge (pp. 26–27).

As I have tried to demonstrate in the preface, our particular lived experiences provide us with only partial interpretations of the world. Without that knowledge of self, we cannot often articulate or recognize the value of difference; rather our partial view allows us only to judge other sources of knowledge as less than. As importantly, when we recognize our limitations, we also can open up to see the world as contradictory and therefore open to dialogue.

COMMUNITY ORGANIZING CONCEPT: SELF-INTEREST

Most teachers enter the profession with a sense of making a difference in the lives of children; however, they are often confronted with incredible challenges and realities about how institutions can best serve children. In his work as a community organizer with the Industrial Areas Foundation (IAF), Chambers (2005) describes binaries that exist between these two worlds—"the world as it is and the world as it should be" (p. 21)—the world in its harsh realities and the world we envision when we talk about justice. In discussing a related binary, Chambers, for example, distinguishes between self-interest and self-sacrifice. In this formulation, self-interest, as opposed to selfish interest, is a necessary condition for penetrating how power works in the "real world." In the early 1900s, Rousmaniere (2005) argued, "Teachers could not begin to think about reform and political activism until they felt empowered to think about themselves. Self-interest, then, was the spark for the progressive political consciousness, but it was also anathema to teachers' professional identity" (p. 36). Educators, particularly within a gendered framework, have often been positioned as nurturing, caring individuals and often are framed within this narrative of self-sacrifice while being discouraged to disregard their own self-interest.

In preparing teachers, then, we must provide future educators with the possibility of examining their self-interest and the difference between public and private—why they do what they do and how are they positioned within complex networks of power and ideology. Working with teacher candidates, I often try to generate conversations that allow them to think deeply about what their commitments are. What does it mean to keep children safe? What does it mean to identify as settler colonists? How can you leave your faith at the door if this is central to who you are? How can we truly recognize all our students without acknowledging the communities from which they come? Perceiving our commitments is grounded in how we engage our own values. We cannot talk about interests without talking about values (Warren, 2001). In talking with teachers and teacher candidates, I would often ask, "What keeps you up at night?" This question was meant to break through the barrage of messages and issues that might be important on their own terms but might not necessarily spark people to act.

Community Organizing Concept: Power

While teachers enact power every day and make decisions about children and young people's lives, I would argue teachers rarely analyze or consider the concept of power. In recent conversations with our National Education Association (NEA) Aspiring Educators liaison, teacher candidates/aspiring educator union members discussed power and how power works when discussing issues around teacher pay. Several teacher candidates expressed how often they had heard from people outside the profession about how noble of them it is to go into teaching and how irritating this was. I countered that I heard many of their peers give up their power saying, "I'm not going into teaching for the money." Teachers have often embodied a spirit of service who may sacrifice their own well-being. As Fretz (2005) has suggested, "When we shrink from power we make a conscious choice to remain isolated and, we implicitly allow things to stay as they are. What we are shrinking from, then, is the responsibility that comes with power and we allow others to make decisions for us rather than engaging ourselves with the real problems of the world" (p. 1).

Teachers may even be hesitant to consider power because of the connotations this word holds. Power suggests control and getting others to do your bidding. As organizer Saul Alinsky (1971) described, "It [the word power] evokes images of cruelty, dishonesty, selfishness, arrogance, dictatorship, and abject suffering. The word *power* is associated with conflict ... Power, in our minds, has become almost synonymous with corruption and immorality" (p. 51). In all of these conceptions, power is something we wield over others often for nefarious purposes and appears to be almost diametrically opposed to how many teachers may view themselves as caring.

When we talk about power within the context of organizing, there is a generative element to the idea of power. For Chambers (2005), power has implications when translated into Spanish where the term "poder" is often defined as being able to do something. As a verb, the term focuses on action. Power is central to the heightening of a public voice, the need for accountability, and the productive aspects of public work. When we consider power in community organizing, we turn to the idea of relational power. Rather than focusing on power over, we focus on power with.

To provide an example, one semester I had a group of teacher candidates who were interested in making a park safer for the kids in the neighborhood. I asked two questions: 1) Do any of you live in this neighborhood? and 2) Do the residents in the neighborhood feel the park is unsafe? Since none of the teacher candidates lived in the neighborhood, they were tasked with interviewing folks in the community. After a couple interviews, the teacher candidates came back and shared that the residents actually felt the park was safe. We have so absorbed the idea that we have a responsibility to make things better for others without recognizing the importance of actually entering into public relationships with folks who are most impacted by particular issues. The idea of relational power requires us to come to know others and to carry out public work together. In order to build these public relationships, organizers rely on individual meetings to understand people's motivation to act in a public capacity.

COMMUNITY ORGANIZING SKILL: INDIVIDUAL MEETINGS

Community organizers emphasize the importance of individual meetings (or relational meetings, one-on-ones, 1:1s) as central to the rebuilding of public institutions. Through these public and personal relationships, people are inspired to create and engage in public work by sharing their hopes and fears as well as their commitments to action. These deep intentional meetings also allow organizers to identify leaders and build powerful networks. As Chambers (2005) has argued:

> The IAF relational meeting is narrow in compass—one person face to face with another—but significant in intention. It is a small stage that lends itself to acts of memory, imagination, and reflection. It constitutes a public conversation on a scale that allows space for thoughts, interests, possibilities, and talent to mix. It is where a public newness begins. A solid relational meeting brings up stories that reveal people's deepest commitments and the experiences that gave rise to them. In fact, the most important thing that happens in good relational meetings is the telling of stories that open a window into the passions that animate people to act (p. 45).

So what are individual meetings? Individual meetings are tightly focused 30-minute meetings that are intended to build lasting public relationships. These meetings are established through credentialing—always referencing why the meeting is taking place and the point of contact—since this helps enlarge a public culture of accountability. If I introduce myself by who has given me that person's name or contact information, I am building on intentional bonds that may exist. It is more likely people will want to meet because of this existing relationship. Relational meetings should seek to make sense of people's stories, their hopes and dreams, their fears, and the actions they have taken. To be respectful of people's time and to ensure the conversations are focused, one-on-one meetings should not pass the 30-minute mark since meetings beyond this point often devolve into private relationships.

After establishing the reason for the meeting (e.g. so and so suggested I meet with you because of your leadership on X), the conversation should be just that—a conversation as opposed to an interview. Start with some general questions—Where are you from? How did you get involved in X? These conversations are followed up with additional questions or more importantly, connections that may lead to a deeper engagement. How do our values shape our commitment? What stories do we tell about why we do what we do? These are all opening to story of our lives and to come to take in the reason why we do what we do, but this is always through stories, not abstractions. But for folks doing individual meetings for the first time, this is where the conversation quickly shifts from natural chit chat when you first meet someone to deep, personal conversations that are prompted by the person leading the meeting. In community organizing, we use "calculated vulnerability" to create a culture of sharing and to open up spaces that are often embedded in superficial small talk. By modelling and sharing our own experiences, we give permission to those in the meeting to share in ways that are personal but also public. But we are also careful not to turn the focus of the meeting away from the person with whom we are talking. Community organizers sometimes use the idea of a 25–75% formula to consider that the person leading the meeting should be speaking about 25% of the time.

To ensure the conversation is both personal and public, community organizers distinguish between probing and prying. Probing engages the person telling their story in helping to examine the motivations for public action, while prying often moves into the realm of the private. When we start asking people about their private relationships or start to heal trauma, we move into a dangerous realm where it is not really our business nor are we equipped as counselors. Chambers (2005) distinguishes between these two, "When people pry, they show excessive curiosity; they try to force the other person open. Curiosity becomes an indiscriminate end in itself. A probe is more focused. It is an attempt to find the other's center. In a relational meeting, probing reveals the underpinnings of someone's public action or inaction" (pp. 50–51). Probes are often meant to deepen and evoke what animated a particular feeling or action and often serve as a way to welcome remembering in ways that allow us to analyze a particular experience. While we are used to a discourse of "niceness" (Castagno, 2019), individual meetings can make folks uncomfortable because people may interrupt and may ask further questions rather than just accepting the answer that are given.

Throughout the meeting, we are paying attention to the motivation for action and considering whether this person is a potential leader. Since we are trying to be conscious of what motivates people to act, we are also interested in prompting some recognition of whether people have acted when they felt something was unjust or needed rectifying. During the course of the individual meeting, organizers engage in agitation—challenging the person to consider why they made a particular decision or chose to act or not act.

Context of Teacher Organizing

Working in conjunction with Northern Arizona Interfaith Council (NAIC), I sought out a grant through the College of Education to be able to lead workshops with teachers. This funding allowed us to pay Northern Arizona Interfaith Council (NAIC) for consultation as well as stipends for teachers who participated in the trainings, conducted individual meetings with parents, and journaled. Through this grant, we were able to work with five teachers, a parent who was also working on principal certification, and the Native American advisor. We asked each participant to attend an individual meeting training, complete three individual meetings with different parents, attend a community organizing training, and complete some journaling related to their engagement. For the first training, we presented educators with some differences between parent involvement and parent engagement (see Chap. 4 for more information). We introduced journals and asked educators to consider how they can involve parents in their classrooms or school and how they might see meetings with parents contributing to their work, and to identify possible parents with whom they might meet.

As a way to identify teachers that would be interested in organizing, I generated a simple question, "Do all parents feel welcome in the school?" If the answer was yes, I moved on to other teachers recognizing the work it would take to bring these teachers on board. If they said, "No" or "Of course not," these became potential leaders in the school. Teachers who recognized the challenges of the school to serve all parents were more cognizant of the realities shaping families and were aware of the impacts of intergenerational trauma and were more likely to have listened to the needs of parents.

To identify parent leadership, we asked teachers to think of parents who had demonstrated leadership but also to be aware of dynamics outside of the school. For example, had parents volunteered in the classroom or for field trips? Had parents shared information about their culture or traditions? Had parents expressed or engaged in ways that were critical of school policies or activities?

After individual meetings, we asked teachers leading the meeting to write down some quick notes. For the purposes of the training, we provided teachers with stick figures of people. What did you learn about the person? What are some events that have shaped who they are? What do they think about? What are their hopes and fears? What are they passionate about? What is in their heart? What actions have they taken? These notes helped to not only keep track of meetings but also serve as a point of reflection about broader issues.

ORGANIZING FOR MUTUAL ACCOUNTABILITY

While Northern Arizona Interfaith Council (NAIC) had been organizing teachers and parents at one of the other elementary schools, I had a chance to see how dynamics between teachers and parents played out. During one workshop, NAIC leaders had wanted to emphasize the joint responsibility teachers and parents could have on curriculum development. The teachers and parents selected based on their leadership were tasked with elaborating a lesson together focused on diversity. The teachers immediately took control of the conversation and generated the activity of creating African masks. There was no consultation with parents, and there was no questioning as to why children in a predominantly Latine and Indigenous school were creating African masks.

In talking with teachers and parents in our first meetings, we asked people to share stories about what was really agitating them. Both groups expressed not feeling appreciated and not knowing one another. Teachers identified their efforts at communicating with parents via letters, newsletters, and notes, but they often found all these notes still in the backpacks. They also wanted parents to show their face in school and being aware of what was happening at school. One of the first-grade teachers who ran the parent pickup expressed frustration with parents who got mad and yelled all kind of things at teachers during car line because parents were in a hurry. The teacher shared, "How do you expect students to follow protocols when parents don't?" Two of the teachers also highlighted home visits. As one of the teachers said, "I have done 19 home visits. Why aren't we a part of their community?" This teacher was committed to visiting different families of her students to get to know the families.

Parents expressed the need for more open communication and wanting to know more clearly what the teachers expected from parents. As one parent expressed, "When do you need help? With what?" Parents expressed how they wanted to feel valued as parents and wanting to feel like partners in the relationship but also wanting to feel like they can make mistakes. One parent said, "We try. We make mistakes. We don't have the degrees to be in those positions." When conversations arose around home visits, parents highlighted the fear of being judged, "I don't pick up toys at 9:00 at night." For a Chicana parent, she expressed the lack of communication from the school. She had given her children's teachers all of her contact information and while she checked her daughter's agenda, no homework was reflected there. When the mother got her daughter's report card, she was surprised that her daughter's report card had gotten lower grades because she had not turned in homework even though the mother kept track of what assignments were due. As one parent highlighted, "I will only believe half of what they tell me if you only believe half of what they tell you." A parent from Ecuador who had started a Montessori school in the Galapagos shared strong reactions about how crowded the classrooms were, kids not wanting to go into the classrooms, and kids not wanting to talk to anyone. He had also expressed how much pent up energy children had and how he saw kids running out of the school at the end of the day. All of these issues had to be prioritized in subsequent meetings to determine what steps to take next.

Community organizers have usually expressed some hesitancy of going into schools. With the inequitable power dynamics that exist between middle-class, predominantly white educators and working-class Communities of Color, the Texas Industrial Areas Foundation (IAF) was one of the first to begin working with schools to address school reform. As Shirley (1997) documents:

> Rather than taking a confrontational approach, Texas IAF leaders emphasized the language of mutual accountability. By developing a more relational approach to schools which accepted the interests and needs of a wide range of community stakeholders, the organization was able to develop legitimacy in the eyes of the many citizens who were alarmed about the low academic achievement of low-income youth (p. 53).

Having established the focus on student coaching around democracy first, we were better positioned to start with an agenda of mutual accountability but also recognized we needed to start with non-curricular issues first because this would pose an immediate threat to teachers who staked out their professional identities. Similar to the Texas IAF which focused on children's safety, we started with mutual concerns from the principal and teachers as well as parents impacted by the lack of transportation for families who lived on the university campus.

Conducting Individual Meetings

As previously mentioned, individual meetings can be challenging for a person leading these for the first time trying to distinguish between interviewing and leading, probing and prying, and generally attempting to identify what values and interests push a person to action. My work with educators was no different.[1] In talking with the principal who had been in and out of trainings but was interested in conducting individual meetings, she was not sure where to start. "What should I talk to the parents about?" Her position of authority made it difficult to envision a role where she could talk to parents about their hopes and fears. Similar to many of the educators, their professional roles made it challenging to have conversations that would allow people to be aware of one another as citizens. Many of the educators used words like "casual" or "interviews" to describe the individual meetings. These words highlight the importance of framing the meetings more intentionally and paying more attention to how we invite stories into these conversations.

For many of the educators, individual meetings remained superficial—what people do and what brought them to Flagstaff, and how parents are involved in their children's education? These are the kinds of questions educators tend to utilize to get to know parents. Educators were able to discuss moving back to Indigenous reservation communities or the challenges military families face. In some cases, educators were able to engage more deeply but faced challenges in trying to move the conversation from the realm of the private to the public arena. In one journal, a teacher wrote about the grandparent with whom she had had a one-on-one: "She speaks a lot about her frustrations w/family, not having the financial support she needs from her daughter to raise her grandkids." She followed this statement with, "I have always been curious about how to help her be more involved as a grandparent, because I think that there are many others in similar situations as her."

For Donna, another teacher, who was involved in conducting home visits, it was difficult to separate her experiences with home visits from this process of leading individual meetings. Rather than individual or relational meetings, she termed these as visits. Rather than focusing on the stories, the teacher spent more time in her journal entries describing the qualities

---

[1] I draw from the individual meeting worksheets and journal entries educators submitted as part of the grant. Institutional Review Board (IRB) was sought for this particular grant and part of the work. Participants signed Informed Consent Forms.

of the person—"committed mother" or "focused and goal-oriented"—or the qualities of the conversation such as "very friendly and easy to talk with."

During one of our conversations about individual meetings, Donna expressed excitement to connect with one of the parents blurring the lines between public and private relationships. As she expressed, "We had so much in common and we ended up talking for two hours during our kids' baseball game." This statement showed me how difficult it was to communicate the differences between public and private relationships. In defining private relationships, Chambers (2005) writes, "[Private relationships] are personal, unique intimate, and many times secret" (p. 73). These relationships are often manifested in how teachers talk about their students, generally framed within individual accounts of how their student succeeded. In contrast, "Standing for the whole—engaging in strong debate, reasoned compromise, and focused action for the common good—requires that we participate in the public domain" (p. 72). Organizers differentiate private relations, best understood as based on loyalty, love, and mutual support, from public relations that are, at best, grounded in respect, accountability, and self-interest (Schutz, 2011, p. 496).

Honoring Community Traditions and Spaces

The individual meetings were an important entry point into thinking about parents and grandparents and their relationships to the school, but I also acknowledge these conversations were too individualistic and did not have enough grounding in the neighborhoods where families lived. Recognizing the need to center community spaces, we initiated a conversation with one of the first-grade teachers. How could we help teachers have knowledge of the communities in which they served? What strengths and needs shaped families' stories and how did this sense of belonging impact the depth of the conversations and stories people shared? As Alinsky (1946) has described:

> The traditions of a people are interwoven in the fabric of their experiences ... It is too ascertain those social forces which argue for constructive democratic action as well as those which obstruct democratic action. To know a people is to know their religions. It is to know the values, objectives, customs, sanctions, and the taboos of these groups. It is to know them not only

in terms of their relationships and attitudes towards one another but also in terms of what relationship all of them have toward the outside (p. 78).

Working with communities required moving outside of the spaces of the school to be able to map the traditions of the community. If we could get teachers outside of the school, we might be able to also get them to think about issues outside of the school.

Through the initiative of this first-grade teacher, Kelly, she organized a neighborhood walk in the housing development across the street. Before the start of the school year, teachers were invited to walk across the street to greet children and their families. While this would not address all the different neighborhoods, this neighborhood walk provided the necessary inroads to get teachers thinking about the opportunities and challenges in different neighborhoods.

Power Mapping, Research, and Identifying Targets

As I narrate in the opening of this chapter, the principal, several of the teachers, and the parents had expressed concerns about attendance. With the closing of schools and the new attendance boundaries, the principal was worried about funding if children who did not start school on the first day of school or who arrived late to school were not counted. Teachers expressed concerns around the disruptions in learning and building community with their classes when children started several weeks after classes had started. A core group of teachers and parents met afterschool to identify and share these concerns. During a series of house meetings (more on these in Chap. 4), parents living in the university family housing expressed concerns about safety and not being able to move in to family housing until several weeks after school had started (because the university started three weeks after the public schools did). The principal had attended several meetings in the family housing community room to listen to the parents about their concerns with having their children walk to school alone, ride the university buses (often not having a place to sit), children running across the street at crosswalks (at the bottom of the hill or by the school), or got lost walking back and forth from school (this issue also surfaced for parents in the housing project almost directly across the street from the school).

Several of the parents lived in family housing at the university so this is where the issue of transportation to and from school surfaced. One parent highlighted seeing kids playing in puddles on the street and students speeding on campus. Another parent highlighted how a university student riding on the shuttle volunteered to help kids on the shuttle. In several follow-up meetings with the transportation director at Northern Arizona University (NAU), parents also identified not having regular shuttles during university breaks, families being locked in when commencement occurred, and shuttles driving right by the elementary school children who were waiting for the shuttle. After identifying several issues, we decided to start with the issue of transportation and general concerns around safety.

In addressing this particular issue, the group had to engage in power mapping to identify individuals who might be involved or should be involved in this conversation. The parents identified potential allies at the university, school board members, and people who may have a direct connection to the issue. This required analyzing institutional hierarchies and organizational charts and recognizing people's motivation for their work. Who would listen and who would care enough to do something? For example, the parents met with the Shuttle Coordinator for the university, but they realized in the meeting this person did not have the power to make any changes. They reached out to the NAU Police Department to see what role if any the campus police had in these conversations. At one point, the group asked, "Are we barking up the wrong tree?" They kept bumping into the people's lack of ability to make these decisions and one of the comments was, "We have to go over people's heads. Who has power over them?"

Conducting research became an iterative process that led to potential new avenues to pursue. The group had to find out about when lights were required for school buses and whether NAU shuttles could be equipped with these, who was allowed to drive these shuttles, who owned the park by the school where the children went in through the fence, and who was responsible for putting up 15 mph school signs on the university campus. The district had also put up roadblocks for this work—federal dollars only cover transportation a mile or more or the bigger buses could not turn around at the top of the hill. The group had to find out about who funded transportation and how these decisions were made. Participants researched walking schools—whereby groups of children would be accompanied by a couple adults—and safe routes to schools.

Identifying targets was also important. While both the university and the school district needed to be part of the conversation, the group was not clear on what would have the most effect. Parents reached out to the university to identify possible solutions—have university buses use similar flashing lights and stop signs, offering crossing guards. The parents who were researching the issue grew increasingly frustrated with NAU and the focus started shifting toward the district.

Brainstorming ideas and producing strategies engulfed the teachers and parents. During our walk described in the opening of this chapter, parents and teachers shared stories of what children experience going to school and back home. On the way down the hill coming back from family housing, the assistant superintendent had already said, "We can make something happen." Through this interaction, the parents and teachers felt the joys of a victory. Even though the district only provided transportation for students in the morning, the ability to advocate for change was exhilarating.

Throughout the rest of the year, parents and teachers would focus on addressing other needs for families living on campus. The group pushed to identify ways in which the university would allow families to move in sooner to coincide with the start of the K-12 school year and a number of other issues related to this particular group of families. Unfortunately, the university had started to make plans to eliminate family housing so many of these other attempts were impacted by the shifting terrain of university expansion.

Lessons Learned

Advancing mutual accountability was an important entry point for the conversation. By starting with an issue that cut across teachers and parents, folks were able to materialize trust across communities that in some ways appeared antagonistic toward one another before the work started. This also allowed parents and teachers to bring in their particular lived experiences, points of contact, and knowledges to the table. Similar to the community organizing literature, folks involved in organizing generate new sensemaking of their institutions and are able to transfer and translate these new understandings into building success for students.

That small victory getting a bus for the families living on the university campus was an important catalyst for organizing work. But that success would not be enough to keep teachers engaged in organizing.

Challenges

In thinking about individual meetings and border crossings, the challenges of trying to break free from the institutional roles we have been trained to carry out are much deeper for white, middle-class educators and educators steeped in ideologies and practices that reinforce individualism and meritocracy. Teacher preparation programs do little in terms of engaging educators meaningfully in community work. The skill sets teachers establish around curriculum, classroom management, and assessment are heavily engrained in an existing pattern of interactions teachers have with families and communities that promote distancing and judgment. How do we help teachers discern and broker the power they have? How can we negotiate new skills sets as democratic professionals? And how do we underscore the importance of involving multiple stakeholders, like parent/guardians as equitable power brokers and district administrators, when needed?

Conclusion

The second year led to an abrupt shift. Soon after we achieved this victory of getting a school bus, the school experienced an assault of mandates that led many of the dedicated teachers to turn their attention away from organizing because of the multiple and frustrating demands from the district. The school's test scores had gone down, and the school was being pressured by the district to take on several new initiatives, which was incredibly frustrating for many of the teachers. Several of the teachers talked about having to learn new technologies and having district officials coming to the school every week to make sure they were implementing new software. The teachers expressed how little time they had and all the teachers who had been part of the training and organizing stopped organizing. While the work stopped with the teachers, the organizing with parents continued. This would also mean that parent organizing would experience much more resistance.

References

Alinsky, S. (1971). *Rules for radicals: A pragmatic primer for realistic radicals.* Vintage Books.
Alinsky, S. D. (1946). *Reveille for radicals.* Vintage Books.

Castagno, A. E. (2019). *The price of nice: How good intentions maintain educational inequity.* University of Minnesota Press.
Castagno, A. E. (2008). "I don't want to hear that!": Legitimating whiteness through silence in schools. *Anthropology & Education Quarterly, 39*(3), 314–333.
Chambers, E. T. (2005). *Roots for radicals: Organizing for power, action, and justice.* Continuum.
Chennault, R. E. (1998). Giving whiteness a black eye: An interview with Michael Eric Dyson. In J. L. Kincheloe, S. R. Steinberg, N. M. Rodriguez, & R. E. Chennault (Eds.), *White reign: Deploying whiteness in America* (pp. 299–328). St. Martin's Press.
Fretz, E. (2005). *Core concept: Power.* Naropa University.
Giroux, H. A. (2005). *Border crossings: Cultural workers and the politics of education* (2nd ed.). Routledge.
Grumet, M. R. (2010). The public expression of citizen teachers. *Journal of Teacher Education, 61*(1-2), 66–76.
Lipsitz, G. (2011). *How racism takes place.* Temple University Press.
Rousmaniere, K. (2005). *Citizen teacher: The life and leadership of Margaret Haley.* State University of New York Press.
Schutz, A. (2011). Power and trust in the public realm: John Dewey, Saul Alinsky, and the limits of progressive democratic education. *Educational Theory, 61*(4), 491–512.
Shirley, D. (1997). *Community organizing for urban school reform.* University of Texas.
Warren, M. (2001). *Dry bones rattling: Community building to revitalize American democracy.* Princeton University Press.
Yosso, T. (2005). Whose culture has capital? A critical race theory discussion of community cultural wealth. *Race, Ethnicity, and Education, 8*(1), 69–91.

CHAPTER 4

The Power of Parent Organizing

Abstract This chapter offers a range of issues impacting families at Transition School to show how parents' voices humanize the context of schools while ensuring public accountability. Distinguishing between parent involvement and parent engagement, I identify the need to conceptualize parents as leaders, allies, and co-creators. I situate the work of education organizing within a Black spatial imaginary and highlight the role of house meetings in bringing public issues to the forefront.

Keywords Black spatial imaginary • Parent involvement • Parent engagement • Public accountability • House meetings

OPENING VIGNETTE

During a house meeting, several of the same Latina mothers shared how their children had been bullied in school. One mother shared a deeply moving and disturbing story about her daughter. The mother found out her daughter had been bullied at school, but it was not until several weeks later. In fact, she only found out because her daughter had developed partial facial paralysis. As the mother narrated the story, she shared how her daughter had been called into the office and was accused of bullying. Her mother was never notified by the teacher or the principal that her daughter was being bullied, and when the daughter raised this with her teacher, the school started coming after the daughter. As the mother cried, several other mothers shared similar stories of finding out their children had been bullied, but the school had not notified them of these incidents. When they approached the principal, the principal said this bullying was being brought into the schools from conflicts happening on the bus and in the neighborhoods; there was nothing they could do about it.

The mothers and I scheduled a meeting with the school counselor. The mothers were clear that the meeting had to be with the counselor and was not to address what had happened but how the school could work with the parents moving forward. The parents wanted to share their stories but only to illustrate how they felt the school could improve on its communication. Since this issue had arisen early on in our organizing and we had not yet fully established full cohesion and leadership, I was apprehensive about the meeting. The issue had impacted some of these mothers in such powerful ways; it seemed important to take a stand. But we still needed more experience having the parents lead the meetings. Were we ready to have this meeting? Did the parents have enough training to lead and navigate the meeting? As we gathered a few minutes before the meeting was supposed to start, I felt the hesitation in the voices of mothers. For some of the mothers, they had experienced outright bullying themselves by the principal or school staff. In a rushed meeting before the school staff showed up, I asked the mothers, "What happens if the principal shows up? Do you all want to cancel the meeting?" With this question, the school counselor and the principal walked in, and we did not have time to make a decision.

I panicked because we had not prepared for this, and I did not know if the mothers would feel comfortable asking the principal to leave or cancelling the meeting. I made a few brief attempts to suggest that the meeting was scheduled with the counselor, but I was not ready to push. The meeting continued with the principal present. We framed the meeting making sure the counselor and the principal understood the mothers were sharing these stories to highlight how they experienced the incidents and to make sure the others understood the goal was how do we move forward.

With that, the meeting started. Everyone introduced themselves, and the parents emphasized as did I that the meeting was to ensure better communication in the future, not to address what happened in the past. Each of the parents then shared their story—bullying on the bus, not being told that their child had been bullied at school, feeling like the school had come after the children or the parents. The meeting became tense quickly with the counselor and the principal pushing back on the stories and said the bullying was being brought into the school from the neighborhoods. As the principal said, and I am paraphrasing, "These kids get into issues at home and then we cannot address it here. They are all cousins or related to one another."

The parents were becoming disheartened, and you could see the same things they had described happening with their kids where the school was not hearing the parents. The principal ended the meeting by saying, "We cannot change what has happened." With that, our meeting ended.

INTRODUCTION

Nationally and locally, Title I schools grapple with how to increase parent engagement in schools. Recognizing that inequalities in power exist between many lower-income families and school counterparts, I address these aspects using a community organizing approach to increase levels of parent engagement (Warren, 2001; Warren et al., 2009). As the narrative above suggests, working-class parents of color may have significantly different perceptions and needs about what they see happening in schools. Community organizing has played an important role in the context of education, particularly when it has sought to create the conditions for parents to be leaders in their schools and communities (Anyon, 2014; Warren et al., 2009). When schools envision parents as co-creators and allies, schools recognize the possibilities for relational power—the building of power with parents (Shirley, 1997, p. 83).

In this chapter, I showcase some of the parent organizing initiatives. To situate this conversation, I begin by contextualizing education organizing. I then explain Black spatial imaginaries, distinguish between parent involvement and parent engagement, and define house meetings and public accountability. The multiple issues identified by parents highlight the breadth and range of issues parents experience. I end this chapter with Lessons Learned along the way.

EDUCATION ORGANIZING

While schools, particularly "underperforming" or "failing" schools, are increasingly asked to focus on narrow definitions of academic achievement, there are efforts underway to link educational institutions to community development. Examples of community organizing—Communities

Organized for Public Service (COPS) in San Antonio and Padres y Jovenes Unidos in Denver—emphasize the importance of organizing parents, students, and teachers in order to bring about meaningful educational reform (Shirley, 1997).

Education organizing serves to bring parents in to make meaning of the governance structures and become attentive to the broader dynamics of the school. Rather than volunteering in classrooms, chaperoning field trips, or attending parent-teacher conferences, which may all be beneficial, parents come to learn about curriculum, lead conversations about safety, or a host of other issues significant to families. More importantly, parents also come to build relationships with staff in schools based on the co-creation of public work and learn to exercise their voice in ensuring accountability.

Marion Orr and John Rogers (2011) have acknowledged the ways in which race, class, and other mediating identities have impacted public engagement because of inequitable participation. As the narrative at the beginning of this chapter and several other examples will highlights, parents have limited opportunities to guide the content or the process of the conversations that take place if they are even encouraged to participate. Orr and Rogers have identified five different streams for public engagement—co-production, democratic governance, community organizing, alliances, and social movements. I focus on community organizing since this model is central to the context of building power and altering spaces to allow for more equitable forms of public engagement. Orr and Rogers describe community organizing as aiming "to build sustained power in the community that can foster mutual and respectful relationships between officials and community members" (p. 16). Unlike political mobilizations, community organizing translates the ongoing maturation of leaders in the community into the long-term building of collective power grounded in deep and ongoing relationships not only with elected officials but also with one another.

BLACK SPATIAL IMAGINARIES

Lipsitz (2011) offers a contrasting view of a Black spatial imaginary. His writing guided me to ask, how can we move beyond the idea of "pure, homogenous spaces" where problems are swept under the rug to spaces that are contested and subject to deliberation? Lipsitz writes:

The Black spatial imaginary views place as valuable and finite, as a public responsibility for which all must take stewardship. Privileging the public good over private interests, this spatial imaginary understands the costs of environmental protection, efficient transportation, affordable housing, public education, and universal medical care as common responsibilities to be shared, rather than as onerous burdens to be palmed off onto the least able and most vulnerable among us (p. 69).

Many of the parents, particularly Parents of Color, with whom I organized demonstrated this different ethic of care. Rather than focusing on sweeping problems under the rug, they envisioned their work as deeply tied to generating public deliberations about issues. Selena, one of the parents, constantly sought to contest normative assumptions about the parents and families. In conversations about fundraising, Selena would always provide ways to engage in ways that allowed for community building and recognizing the community assets. She challenged parents to consider how fundraising campaigns to sell gift wrapping paper had little to do with many of the working-class families in the school. Instead, she suggested organizing dinners and *fiestas* where families could come, folks could learn how to make different foods, and most importantly build community and solidarity. Her attempts to address special education, parent engagement, or curriculum were all embedded within a larger social fabric of visioning a school that acknowledged the presence of diverse communities. Edwin, another Latino parent, expressed concerns about the obedience and conformity the school sought to establish in both individual and group meetings. Expressing the need for movement and greater creativity, he worked to acknowledge the repression students face collectively of their curious minds and bodies.

Whiteness tends to normalize and universalize experiences, thus perpetuating an appearance of unity. Tension is a necessary part of public life, and it is only through this tension between the need to advocate for the change and the desire for unity that we identify our public responsibility (Chambers, 2005). To envision our collective sense of responsibility, we must break out of individualistic notions central to the dominant culture. As you will see in the next section, parent engagement recognizes the potentiality of parents to be leaders and to acknowledge our only interest may not be the needs of our individual child.

DISTINGUISHING BETWEEN PARENT INVOLVEMENT AND PARENT ENGAGEMENT

Traditionally, parent involvement and the criteria for this are established by the school. Parent-teacher conferences, parent nights, reading to children at night are some examples by which schools establish expectations and then measure whether the parental involvement is adequate. For Title I schools, schools may struggle with parental involvement under these criteria. Epstein et al. (1997) have generated a framework of six types of involvement that would be beneficial in forming partnerships. These include parenting, communicating, volunteering, learning at home, decision-making, and collaborating with community. The first four are unidirectional whereby the school communicates its expectations to families and provides mechanisms to support these. The fifth and sixth types of involvement allow parents to be engaged in decisions about the school or the community, but the flow of information still relies on moving from school to families.

In seeking to distinguish parental involvement from parental engagement, I hope to build on the literature that recognizes parents and families and co-creators and citizens. Shirley (1997) has distinguished between these two concepts:

> Parental *involvement*—as practiced in most schools and reflected in the research literature—avoids issues of power and assigns parents a passive role in the maintenance of school culture. Parental *engagement* designates parents as citizens in the fullest sense—change agents who can transform urban schools and neighborhoods (p. 73).

Drawing on the community organizing literature and practices that emphasize leadership development, parent engagement frames participation as based on identifying parent concerns, building deep mutual relationships, and strengthening a collective base of empowerment for parents to fully engage in the life of the school (Warren et al., 2009). As parents participate as citizens, they deepen their beliefs on how to support their children because they begin to analyze power and the potential they have to transform their own relationships to schools (Ferlazzo & Hammond, 2009).

In highlighting important differences between parent involvement and parent engagement, Ferlazzo and Hammond (2009) have identified how schools might elicit ideas, hopes, and dreams as a way of formulating stronger relationships built on trust and as a way of inviting parents into participating in ways that are meaningful and relevant to the parents' needs. Within this formulation, parents act as leaders while educators can serve as organizers and thus can create a joint vision. As I discovered in the work of organizing at the elementary school, school staff felt fearful that they would lose power seeing it as a zero-sum game. In a parent engagement model, Ferlazzo and Hammond describe the partnership as "broad and deep" because the partnerships allow schools to tackle issues in the community (p. 10).

COMMUNITY ORGANIZING CONCEPT: PUBLIC ACCOUNTABILITY

The public sphere, organizers argue, is a realm of conflicts over power and resources. The central aspect of public relations is not trust but *accountability* (Schutz, 2011, p. 497).

As community organizers often point to, public officials tend to try to establish private relationships to avoid being held publicly accountable. By introducing themselves by their first names, public officials can try to minimize the distance with constituents to build a false sense of trust (Chambers, 2005). Privatizing relationships creates a false sense of trust based on intimacy but erodes our ability to require accountability.

When I was working with the National Education Association Aspiring Educators union chapter executive board (Chap. 6), we experienced this issue of an absence of accountability. Executive board members had created such tight-knit communities based on private relationships, we lost the ability to hold ourselves accountable to the organization, each other, and ourselves. Conflict should have been much more visible, but because of these friendships, folks were afraid to call each other out. While I did not ask leaders to step away, I asked some of the leaders to get out of the way. Resolving personal situations occupied the majority of the meeting time and prevented meaningful work from being accomplished.

I initially worked to build trust between parents and educators because of the deep chasms of trust manifested in their sense of expectations for each other. However, when teachers stood side by side with parents around an issue of mutual concern, the accountability in the success weighed more heavily than any words could accomplish. I realized trust comes after accountability when we are engaged in the creation of public work.

COMMUNITY ORGANIZING SKILL: CONDUCTING HOUSE MEETINGS

In order to create connections with one another and to build collective understandings of issues, we used house meetings to organize parents, teachers, and neighborhood groups. In community organizing, we will follow up with potential leaders with whom we have met in individual meetings. If folks have expressed excitement and energy and may have a large following because they are perceived as leaders, we invite these individuals to set up a house meeting with their neighbors. This process was incredibly important to allow parents to share stories and identify common issues as well as how they might tackle these issues. Shirley (1997) has argued, "House meetings have many important facets. One of the most important of those involves a shift from a culture of civic withdrawal and self-blaming to a culture of conversation and the public processing of pain" (p. 61). Applying this idea to the context of schools, parents have a chance to connect outside of the realms of their private relationships. By sharing stories in public, we start to recognize the public dimensions of our identities and begin acknowledging the commitments we have to one another.

House meetings have a general structure that allows for the processing of experiences. The generation of stories also allows people to create connections around similar issues. After introductions, people would be encouraged to share stories. The stories are not pre-determined nor are people identified around a particular issue. Through the process of hearing the stories, we sometimes find ourselves coalescing around a shared set of stories or we may find ourselves generating multiple issues. In house meetings, similar to individual meetings, we may try to identify what energy exists around a specific issue and follow up with a separate meeting to consider how to move forward with that particular issue.

Paralleling the structure of individual meetings, organizers need to push people away from abstractions or issues affecting other people since these conversations take up space; organizers may often probe specific ideas to help generate how a particular issue is affecting a person or people. In our model of organizing at Transition School with parents, house meetings tended to focus on issues in or around the school, but Industrial Areas Foundations (IAF) tends to organize a broad array of issues that may extend outside of schools including immigration, affordable housing, health care, or any other set of issues. Through this process of listening to stories, organizers have a chance to identify other potential leaders and schedule individual meetings. As I will show below, house meetings can be organized around affinity groups or across groups in what social capital theorists called bridging and bonding spaces.

Bridging and Bonding Spaces

In 2010, a good friend and the afterschool coordinator of the 21st Century Grant which funds afterschool reading and math support, asked me, "Gerald, can you translate for parents tonight? The principal asked me to invite the Latine parents tonight and I need to go over the guidelines of the program." "Sure, I say." This provided an important entry point into getting to know Latine parents and continuing the work of organizing parents at the school.

In retrospect, I would think about organizing differently strategically considering the need for both building and bonding spaces. While our organizing started around the idea of neighborhoods (and we were successful in one particular community to extend shared conversations among neighbors and had the principal attend many of these meetings), unexpected events such as translating for the Latine parents shifted how we unfolded our approach to house meetings. Since I had translated for families and helped organize English classes at the school, many Latine leaders came from these spaces, but I had also met parents at university housing and through organizing efforts outside of the school.

The process started to shift to focus on different identity groups as a way to acknowledge the different lived experiences and issues that arose as well as my own positionality and connection to particular communities. For predominantly white parents with students in special education, issues tended to revolve around the ways in which their children were served by new models of whole-class, data-driven parent-teacher conferences. For Indigenous families, recognizing and implementing more cultural events reflecting their cultural backgrounds seemed more central. Latine parents, on the other hand, identified a range of issues including bullying, curriculum, and translation. Social capital theory highlights the role of bridging and bonding spaces (Kirkby-Geddes et al., 2013; Putnam, 2020).

However, recognizing the distinct nature of the different conversations and the different levels of relationship and engagement on my part, bonding spaces around ethnic identities or neighborhood connections were absolutely necessary for parents to recognize the shared histories and experiences. Bonding spaces are spaces that allow folks with shared identities to come together to be able to strengthen their sense of community and solidarity.

While we were able to cultivate bonding spaces for Latine parents and started some of this work with Indigenous parents, the lack of articulation across shared interests also reduced our power to articulate a larger collective vision. Bridging space is necessary for building collective power across different affinity groups.

STORIES FROM PARENT ORGANIZING

In sharing the following stories, I provide a range of issues parents experience and the spaces where we organized. I also bring to light the specific ways in which these issues connect to a larger tradition of IAF organizing and how the organizing shaped my understandings of what we needed to do to become effective organizers.

Identifying Parent Leaders

I do not recall how I first met Selena, a natural leader, but it was soon after the start of school. This firebrand Chicana mom with four children had come from Chicago public school system and she knew special education law. During one of our first conversations, Selena shared that she had been calling the school to make sure her children at the school were evaluated for special education services within the timeline required by law. She said no one had gotten back to her so she was getting ready to sue the school. Selena understood her rights and how to hold people accountable.

Selena gravitated naturally to the idea of community organizing. She understood and advocated for her children daily, but she also envisioned a broader responsibility to all children. In an early conversation with the principal, the principal said, "Do not ever leave me alone in a room with Selena!" She was terrified of Selena and also positioned through a deficit lens. The principal said, "Selena just needs to take care of her kids. You know she has enough on her plate with three of her kids in special education." I wondered how the principal felt so comfortable sharing a comment like that with me. Selena, however, had the heart of an organizer. She understood her responsibility to fight for all kids.

As IAF organizers have generally recognized, "An angry parent is an opportunity" (cited in Anyon, 2014, p. 174). Parents who have been marginalized often have the ability to break through the dominant paradigm because they understand the ways in which exclusion works. Much of the work of organizers is helping translate "hot anger" into "cold anger" (Rogers, 1990). In defining cold anger, Rogers is moved to describe it as follows: "Rather, it is an anger that seethes at the injustices of life and transforms itself into a compassion for those hurt by life. It is an anger rooted in direct experience and held in collective memory. It is the kind of anger that can energize a democracy—because it can lead to the first step in changing politics" (pp. 9–10). Hot anger can destroy us leaving us feeling bitter and self-involved. However, when we can translate that anger into cold anger, we use anger as a source to strategically and collectively bring pressure to a situation as a way to rectify injustice and contempt.

Parent-Teacher Organization (PTO)

These PTO meetings were generally small with maybe four or five parents and the principal, no teachers were usually present, and the parents were all white. While conversations usually revolved around fundraising ideas or organizing a breakfast or luncheon for teachers, the few working-class parents who had attended meetings and not been heard had stopped coming.

After conducting house meetings with Latine parents to identify issues of concern, 12 Latine parents attended the next PTO meeting. When the usual parents saw the Latine parents come in, the PTO president quickly said to me, "Maybe you can translate for the parents in that corner while we conduct the meeting." I responded, "But you actually have more parents that speak Spanish, and they cannot actually participate. We can translate the entire meeting." The PTO president responded, "But that would make the meeting really long."

At the next meeting, the PTO president tendered her resignation saying, "I don't like the direction we are headed." Challenging the hegemonic claims to English-only, the new board president was bilingual and was excited to run the meetings in English and Spanish and went a step further by translating PTO newsletters and information. Unfortunately, this presidency was short-lived because the parent became too busy with work and had to step down several months later.

Math Curriculum

During a house meeting with several Latine mothers, a number of parents brought up the issue of math instruction. Several of the mothers identified that their children appeared to be behind in math and expressed concern about the limited time teachers spent on math. One mother, a teacher from Mexico, who was here in Flagstaff with her husband on his sabbatical, led the conversation about how they might be able to work with their children to learn math concepts. Several of the mothers echoed the importance of math from their own schooling in Mexico, and this generated a need to push harder around math.

As this example highlights, parents were deeply involved in their children's education and this group of parents had a good pulse of what was happening in the school around academics. The principal had shown an interest in having the parents work more closely with their children to support them academically. Like in many schools, parent nights were often dedicated to telling parents about the importance of supporting their children's learning. One parent night had showcased the importance of reading to your children and identified the research around the number of words children were exposed to at different socio-economic levels to make the case that parents should be reading to their children every night.

However, in approaching the principal about math instruction, the principal appeared more reticent to support the parents in their quest to make math instruction more rigorous. Can parents get access to the math curriculum for the district? Can parents get copies of the math book pages so they can work with their kids at home? Can parents get extra workbooks? For each of these questions, the principal just kept saying, "No." While we never understood why, this hesitation seemed to contradict the position the principal always shared publicly around her focus on parent involvement. Was it a fear of losing control? Would it undermine the authority of the teachers or the principal? Would this require admitting that teachers were not spending enough time on math?

Within the context of the Texas IAF, Shirley (1997) documents the various reasons why principals may be resistant to change (p. 225). Without community organizing skills, parents may bring in questions or suggestions that deviate from teachers' expectations and training or may advocate for positions to favor their own children at the expense of other children. While middle-class parents may often have significant clout in schools, organized working-class parents could threaten the authority or job security of the principal. Organized parents can also challenge the authority of the district as was the case in Texas.

Parent and Family Involvement Team

The school had asked me to identify and reach out to parents to be part of the Parent and Family Involvement Team for their Success for All framework. After several months of organizing and talking with parents about their hopes and dreams, we had a number of parents that had identified issues that were impacting their families. I reached out to several of these parents to attend this meeting.

For the first 30 minutes of this hourlong meeting, the teachers were discussing what students could wear on Friday since it was Valentine's Day, and the teachers wanted to create fun engagement on that day. Kelly, one of the teachers, expressed, "If the girls wear pink, what color can the boys wear?"

As the meeting progressed, my exasperation mounted and the parents probably wondered why they were at the meeting, I asked the teachers if the parents could share their concerns. The parents came with two concerns—letters being sent to families who were being reported for more than ten unexcused absences and the format of the parent-teacher conferences, which had particularly impacted students receiving special education supports.

Since there was only 30 minutes left in the meeting and teachers kept discussing what to do for Valentine's Day for several more minutes, we only had a chance to discuss the first issue shared by the parents. Three of the parents expressed they had received letters from the school suggesting their names would be forwarded to the county attorney for possible criminal action since their children had more than ten unexcused absences. Working-class parents expressed fear of having to deal with this on top of whatever else they were experiencing. As one parent said, "My child doesn't want to come to school every morning, and it is a fight to get him out of the car." In the case of another parent, she expressed that the school already knew about her child's situation owing to a medical condition. One of the only male teachers, who was a leader in the school, spoke up and said, "Parents should not have to deal with this. We already have documented what is happening." But other teachers expressed there was nothing they could do saying, "It is the law." I suggested translating for parents was also the law, but the school generally disregarded this and this comment was met with silence.

While there was not enough time to engage in this next conversation about parent-teacher conferences, this was another issue that the parents who attended this committee meeting had wanted to share. The school had recently moved to a new model for parent-teacher meetings to provide feedback based on Maria Paredes' work at WestEd with the Academic Parent-Teacher Teams (APTT) (*Family Engagement – Academic Parent-Teacher Teams (APTT)*, n.d.). For this model, the classroom teacher meets with all the parents three times during the year and provides folders showing how each child compared to other children in the classroom based on data. In addition, the model encourages one individual meeting with parents to build relationships even though the school also allowed or encouraged teachers to meet with parents individually as needed. For parents with children with disabilities, this model was devastating. As one of the parents shared with me individually, "I already know my child cannot do as well as the other kids in his class, but now I have to sit there and see how badly they do in comparison to every other kid in the class."

To organize for mutual accountability, we needed to jointly create the agenda. The teachers had their own sets of concerns that did not mirror the more pressing concerns expressed by parents. The parents were being invited into a space that was not jointly created and therefore not co-owned. Before entering this space, we had to recreate this space in a way that acknowledged the Parent and Family Involvement Team.

Fry Bread Sale

During one of my few meetings with only Indigenous parents, mostly Navajo parents expressed how they would want to see more of their culture reflected in the school. Every year the school celebrated one day by making fry bread and having a cultural event. While this varied in scope, the parents felt there was not enough focus on Indigenous cultures. The parents gravitated toward the idea of raising money for cultural events. By creating funding, the parents believed the school would be more willing to bring in more Indigenous-centered events. With this focus, several of the meetings revolved around organizing a fundraiser selling Navajo tacos (these are made with fry bread rather than tortillas).

Soon after the fundraiser, I started receiving indirect messages from the principal. She would send these through the afterschool program coordinator. "Gerald, these separate meetings for Native American parents are racist because you are segregating parents." Even though the school had a Native American advisor for a couple of days a week recognizing the distinct needs of Indigenous communities, this notion that we were segregating parents became a continuous comment I would hear indirectly from the principal through various comments to other people. Interestingly, I was asked to translate for Latine parents for the afterschool program orientation, and the subsequent house meetings did not seem to attract the same kind of comments even though this work had been much more critical, impactful, and continuous.

Lessons Learned

As an organizer without the seasoning of more experienced organizers, I was committed to surfacing issues important to the parents. However, it was sometimes easier to try to talk directly with the principal rather than taking the time to build the skill sets with parents. The IAF focuses on the trifecta of research, action, and evaluation (Chambers, 2005). We identified issues but needed more dedicated time to researching, organizing actions, and critically reflecting on these. Looking back on all of these examples suggests I should have focused on fewer issues and worked more on honing the public skills of the parents through specific actions. As Chambers (2005) has stated, "The intentional discipline of IAF requires that public actions begin and end in reflection. While no one develops a public life without action, we only learn how to build the power to act for justice in the real world when public actions are preceded and followed by disciplined reflection" (p. 15). For Saul Alinsky (1971), the purpose of every action was to get a reaction. If parents had been told "no" each time they made a proposal, this anger would have proved to be a catalyst that would have encouraged us to think through our actions in more deliberate ways while also acquiring the necessary skills.

As an organizer, I needed to build up the leadership capacity to carry out the meeting about bullying with just the counselor. This required widening the skills to set the agenda, facilitate the meeting, and push back all necessitated spaces to learn and practice these skills. The parents and I needed to be able to say we will not meet if the principal stayed, and we needed to be able to keep the meeting focused on parents' needs. As Chambers (2005) highlights, "In public life, politeness is not civility; it's the sin of the middle class yearning to join the ranks of the haves. It is the refuge of those who have not developed their political capacity to the point where they can stand the tension and heat of controversy" (p. 34). I realized I had to unlearn my own class privilege and follow the lead of parents like Selena who could not depend on politeness to advocate for their children.

Conclusion

When teachers and parents were organizing together during our first year, I recognized the power and ability of teachers and parents to talk across different contexts and needs. Through these conversations, both groups were able to recognize each other's needs and work together to come up with solutions. We were most effective when teachers were part of the organizing, but I want to highlight that these interactions also required a shared acknowledgment that was not always present, thus limiting the ability of parents to bring to light the other conversations we had around specific cultural issues and challenges.

Within the more specific context of schools, most teachers still occupy a privileged position that does not always recognize the power of teachers to serve as border crossers. When working only with parents, I realized the unrecognized needs of parents for translation, for a more rigorous curriculum, for cultural relevance, and for a greater understanding of the challenges facing families often go unacknowledged because of the dissonance of these experiences with educators who work in schools. Working-class Parents of Color do not generally have a seat at the decision-making table nor are educators willing to give up the little decision-making power they do have.

Parent organizing can create the conditions and tools to allow families to surface and channel their concerns. While we saw examples of collaboration when teachers were involved, parents may need to exert pressure, build power, and make demands if they are going to be acknowledged fully.

References

Alinsky, S. (1971). *Rules for radicals: A pragmatic primer for realistic radicals.* Vintage Books.

Anyon, J. (2014). *Radical possibilities: Public policy, urban education, and a new social movement* (2nd ed.). Routledge.

Chambers, E. T. (2005). *Roots for radicals: Organizing for power, action, and justice.* Continuum.
Epstein, J., Coates, L., Salinas, K. C., Sanders, M. V., & Simon, B. S. (1997). *School, family, and community partnerships: Your handbook for action.* Corwin Press.
Family Engagement – Academic Parent-Teacher Teams *(APTT).* (n.d.). WestEd. Retrieved June 6, 2021, from https://www.wested.org/service/family-engagement-academic-parent-teacher-teams
Ferlazzo, L., & Hammond, L. (2009). *Building parent engagement in schools.* Linworth.
Kirkby-Geddes, E., King, N., & Bravington, A. (2013). Social capital and community group participation: 'Bridging' and 'bonding' in the context of a healthy living centre in the UK. *Community & Applied Social Psychology,* 271–285. https://doi.org/10.1002/casp.2118
Lipsitz, G. (2011). *How racism takes place.* Temple University Press.
Orr, M., & Rogers, J. (Eds.). (2011). *Public engagement for public education: Joining forces to revitalize democracy and equalize schools.* Stanford University Press.
Putnam, R. D. (2020). *Bowling alone: The collapse and revival of the American community* (20th Anniversary ed.). Simon & Schuster Paperbacks.
Rogers, M. B. (1990). *Cold anger: A story of faith and power politics.* University of North Texas Press.
Schutz, A. (2011). Power and trust in the public realm: John Dewey, Saul Alinsky, and the limits of progressive democratic education. *Educational Theory, 61*(4), 491–512.
Shirley, D. (1997). *Community organizing for urban school reform.* University of Texas.
Warren, M. (2001). *Dry bones rattling: Community building to revitalize American democracy.* Princeton University Press.
Warren, M. R., Hong, S., Leung Rubin, C., & Sychitkokhong Uy, P. (2009). Beyond the bake sale: A Community-based relational approach to parent engagement in schools. *Teachers College Record, 111*((9), 2209–2254.

CHAPTER 5

The Power of Student Organizing: Public Achievement

Abstract This chapter offers a portrait of how I came to understand and implement Public Achievement, coaching elementary school students about democracy. Through contextualizing Public Achievement and the centrality of public work, I share examples of this work and also describe structural limitations we faced to highlight the importance of embeddedness of this work in the everyday work of teachers as curriculum developers and justice-oriented educators.

Keywords Public Achievement • Public work • Everyday politics

OPENING VIGNETTE

The eight first and second graders included white, Latine, Indigenous (Navajo and Hopi), and one Arabic-speaking student for our second Public Achievement (PA) team meeting. We stepped outside into the hallway for our team-building activity. As the children stand in the hallway, I ask students to say hello in any language they speak. "Hi." "Hola." "Yá'át'ééh." "As-salaam 'alykum." The girl who speaks Arabic fidgets nervously as she giggles uncontrollably. "I have never spoken Arabic in school before." We return to the class where we had formed a big rectangle with the little desks. I asked the children to introduce themselves in whatever language they would like and encourage them to identify their clans (if appropriate). As the conversation ensues and children start talking to one another, a Hopi boy says, "He is making fun of my clans." I start to recognize the children have had little exposure and ability to share important parts of their backgrounds.

For the next meeting, I brought in books from the library to start generating more concrete ideas of who and how each of the students might be reflected culturally in the school. How do we start creating new relationships that are culturally mediated and responsive to the different communities in the school? How can books and stories about the children who are reflected on our PA team allow misconceptions to be articulated and challenged? And what would it look like to generate a school space that is reflective of these multiple communities?

We reach out to parents to ask for their help to translate key places in the school into their home languages. I wonder how can we ask these larger questions with our eager students who have little access to these conversations? How do they come to wonder about the broader context of language and culture when multiple languages and culture are not embraced in the school?

I started coaching this group because we did not have enough coaches to meet with the different teams; I was excited to explore what might be possible. Several of the projects over the course of the three semesters had tended to devolve into creating posters about saving the Earth or stop bullying without efforts to really engage in what Public Achievement entailed—the creation of public work and the development of specific skills necessary for public work—identifying self-interests, working across differences, researching, utilizing power maps to identify potential stakeholders that could actually help make whatever changes possible. What would it look like to invite parents as collaborators to encourage their children to think about multilingual spaces? How might the labelling of different places around the school in multiple languages that reflected the families present in school create new possibilities for envisioning the beauty of this public school as a representation of diverse racial, ethnic, and tribal communities in the United States?

Introduction

As the opening story suggests, children and young people in school may have limited access to engaging their full selves. Traditionally, youth have had little representation or participation in voicing their community concerns or engaging in actions to address these concerns. In this context, youth have been portrayed as uninterested in civic engagement, deviant, and increasingly criminal (Noguera, 2003). When asking young people what concerns they had in Minneapolis, MN, as part of envisioning a Public Achievement, youth documented hundreds of issues challenging the widespread misconceptions that young people do not care. In follow-up questions, youth were asked what they could do about these issues, and the response was "Nothing." This work challenged the political science literature that young people were apathetic recognizing more so that young people were discouraged with traditional politics (Harris et al., 2010).

In this chapter, I begin by briefly historicizing Public Achievement (PA). I introduce two central concepts for Public Achievement—public work and every day politics—to offer an approach to engaging youth. I then highlight how we implemented Public Achievement in two schools and provide an example of how we carried out PA. I end with Lessons Learned and consider how this work might be fully integrated into the everyday work of teachers.

Public Achievement

In 1990, Public Achievement (PA) was started through the University of Minnesota's Humphrey Institute in partnership with the then mayor of St. Paul, Minnesota, as a way to explore how to engage youth in politics (Boyte, 2004). By asking youth to describe the problems in their schools and communities, the Center for Democracy and Citizenship sought to generate a model that would provide young people with a way to be active participants in public life (*Public Achievement*, n.d.). Drawing on its roots in the citizenship schools during the Civil Rights Movement and community organizing models, PA reconceptualizes politics. Through PA, young people are conceptualized as active participants and decisionmakers, who are co-creators of a democratic way of life and have the ability and power to posit solutions around everyday problems and concerns impacting their lives, their schools, and their communities. As Boyte (2008) describes:

The framework in Public Achievement stresses a different kind of politics, co-creative politics that revolves around diverse citizens' needs, interests, and capacities, and that teaches the skills and habits of working with people who differ from one another... In Public Achievement, young people are conceived as co-creators, citizens today, not simply citizens-in-waiting. They help to build democracy in their schools, neighborhoods, and society (p. 15).

Public Achievement provides a concrete model to identify a number of issues confronting young people in society, but more importantly, the tools to systematically respond to these issues with a range of tools that allow young people to participate in the civic life of their schools and communities.

COMMUNITY ORGANIZING CONCEPT: PUBLIC WORK

Central to Public Achievement is the concept of public work. PA puts great faith in the ability of everyday citizens to co-create an enlarged civic space. Kari (2007) describes:

> public work is defined as the visible, sustained efforts of a diverse mix of people that produce goods—material or cultural—of lasting civic value. Citizens are thus cocreators and producers, not only bearers of rights and responsible members of communities. Public work points to the *productive* not just the *distributive* side of politics, thus defining politics as about creating and building communities and, more broadly, as a democratic way of life (p. 24).

Unlike social movements and protest politics, public work rejects strong ideological positions and divisive cultural politics. By focusing on what people can build together in their local communities, PA establishes common ground—the need for a stop sign, the retooling of abandoned lots, or the cleaning up of communities.

In distinguishing between liberal, communitarian, and public work approaches to democracy, Boyte (2004) highlights the centrality of public work in bringing people together as producers and co-creators of a democratic way of life (p. 93). Challenging both the notion of voters and volunteers, Boyte argues public work moves away from stagnant political processes and from the idea of creating dependencies that do little to solve the root cause of problems. For example, conversations about food insecurity lead to discussions of whether the government should provide social safety nets or whether food banks can help ameliorate hunger.

COMMUNITY ORGANIZING CONCEPT: EVERYDAY POLITICS

Unlike traditional politics that focuses on democracy as voting and representation, Boyte (2004) argues for an everyday politics. In traditional politics, citizenship is not a daily exercise but rather a ritual that has led to considerable apathy. As we can see, these ritual enactments are entrenched "habits" where people uncritically and unquestioningly make decisions based on an already established set of beliefs. This traditional politics is entrenched in deep polarizations where people win or lose based on a simple majority, discussions are in reality arguments where listening and learning do not actually change positions. This is what PA would call the distributive side of politics of who gets what in a simple zero-sum game.

In everyday politics, citizens enact these identities by participating actively in identifying problems and finding solutions in their local communities. As Boyte (2004) states, "Everyday politics, in the sense used and argued for here, requires learning the skills of negotiation among diverse interests among citizens or relatively equal standing, across partisan and other divisions, to accomplish tasks or to solve problems" (p. 37). These practices are the cornerstone of democratic societies and also require an ongoing, deliberative attention to our neighbors and communities. By working to have knowledge of one another, we generate the creative capacity to envision new ways of looking at a particular problem and identifying a wider range of possibilities to address the problem.

PUBLIC ACHIEVEMENT IN ACTION

First graders sit in a circle crisscross applesauce. Public Achievement coaches elicit conversations about the core concepts of power and freedom. First graders eagerly raise their hands to answer the question: What does freedom mean? Not being grounded. Being able to choose. Who has power? Spiderman, light bulbs. In the space of seconds, every child provides an idea. Suddenly, one girl says, "We do. We have power because we are free." Over the course of eight to ten weeks, elementary school students work with their coaches to identify a problem and examine an issue in their school or community; acquire the language of democracy, citizenship, power, public work, freedom, and self-interest; and learn to conduct a power analysis to note the resources available to them to map out strategies.

Context of Public Achievement Northern Arizona University (NAU)

In 2009, two of my colleagues at NAU had attended a conference and were introduced to the idea of Public Achievement. Through their engagement with the Sustainable Communities program, they had cultivated a partnership with Community School,[1] one of the local elementary schools. Through the Masters in Sustainable Communities and some funding from the Community, Culture and Environment Endowed Chair, the partnership relied on the training of graduate students to serve as facilitators for a range of community partnerships including Public Achievement.

As the program was promoted at Community School, the intention was to situate Public Achievement in the afterschool program to expose teachers and students to the model. Eventually, the goal was to have classroom teachers include Public Achievement as part of the everyday curriculum. The principal and afterschool coordinator were excited to incorporate PA into the school because of their both personal and professional connections to NAU. The afterschool coordinator was connected to one of the faculty who saw the presentation on PA and brought it to Flagstaff. The principal saw an opportunity to partner with NAU to bring in new ideas.

While this aspect of making Public Achievement part of the daily curriculum never materialized, we had a similar vision for Transition School. The afterschool coordinator at Transition School attended the trainings at Community School and was excited to bring the program to her school. Working through the 21st Century federal grant, the afterschool program consisted in supporting students in literacy and/or math. Most of the teachers were classroom teachers who stayed afterschool. When the grant came up for renewal, PA was written into the grant.

In order to support these efforts at both schools, we created a First Year Seminar around Public Achievement at NAU. This class was geared toward first-year college students interested in doing fieldwork in elementary schools. Our college students, who PA calls coaches, had to juggle learning key concepts around PA while also engaging K-5 students in implementing action plans. Working with some incredible graduate students who were also teaching assistants and later faculty, we worked to strengthen a structure to support PA coaches. During the course, we introduced

---

[1] A pseudonym for a school located in the geographic center of a predominantly Latine and Indigenous working-class community impacted by ICE raids and heavily focused on providing a range of services and conversations for these communities.

coaches to key concepts, public narratives, individual meetings, cycle of community organizing, conducting a power analysis, identifying issues, and team-building skills. As we gained some experience with the course, we also started to include more concrete examples—panels of coaches from prior semesters, a tour of the school with a Q&A, and community mapping activities to coaches so that they would be able to connect to the community outside of the school. The course structure moved from more theoretical to more practical as we taught the classes over the semesters, particularly as we created additional expectations that coaches had to be conscious of how to lesson plan to align more closely with the teachers with whom they worked. Since we had to also include a focus on literacy and math skills, we hoped teachers whom worked with university students would integrate PA into their school curriculum. Below I provide some context around how we implemented Public Achievement at Transition School.

Engaging Public Achievement

Over the course of each semester, our first-year college student coaches would usually have two weeks in their college classroom before going into schools. During these two weeks, we introduced coaches to key concepts while also providing them with time to brainstorm the first couple weeks in the school. During this time, we modeled team-building activities and also encouraged coaches to conduct individual meetings with the teachers with whom they would be coaching. As we strengthened relationships and had the opportunity to connect with coaches, we introduced tours of the school, panels by former coaches, and created maps of the community around the school so coaches would have some knowledge of the community. During the third week, we had coaches go in to shadow their teachers on the one day of the week they would be coaching so they would be familiar with the dynamics of the afterschool program as well as promoted a sense of the expectations teachers had for the space.

Public Achievement maps out Six Stages (*The Six Stages of Public Achievement*, n.d.). These stages include: Exploration and Discovery, Issue Development, Problem Research, Designing a Project, Implementing the Action Plan, and Reflection/Communication/Celebration. As I highlight later, one of the tensions was trying to accomplish all of this over an eight- to ten-week time frame. I provide some context for each of the stages below as we utilized these.

During the first couple weeks, we focused on the Exploration and Discovery stage. We encouraged coaches and teachers to do some team-building to get to know students, identify interests, and generate a space that often allowed for more democratic deliberation including rules or agreements. Sometimes these conversations challenged the existing models teachers used and we had to figure out ways to carve out a different space for PA time. During these first couple of weeks, coaches would often engage students in walking around the school or when possible around the neighborhood. Students would take pictures of things they saw in their school or neighborhood or draw pictures. These pictures of drawings were intended to serve as a starting place for what issues were most important. Through these, students often identified trash on the playground or around the school, issues around bullying, access to water fountains during recess, or a range of other issues often focused on the idea of concrete and visible work. We often tried to stay away from issues far away such as saving the polar bears or issues that impacted individual students such as substance abuse facing parents (since this often required a different kind of intervention and support).

Once students had identified potential issues, coaches moved students into the Issue Development stage. In our early attempts, we held true to the idea of an Issues Convention where students deliberated on the various issues and weighed the pros and cons of different issues. While this is a critical stage, we often found coaches tended to not give this particular focus enough time. We encouraged coaches to grasp the various aspects of the issues before they made decisions with students. However, with the push to implement action plans and the short timeline, the conversations did not always yield the needed complexity.

Once the students had decided on the issue, they were guided to think about Problem Research. In order to identify the problem they would address, students had to consider different aspects of the issue to figure out where they might focus their attention. For example, for one team, they identified the issue of not having access to water while outside on the playground or on the field. Students needed to wait until they came back in after recess to drink water or they would have to have a teacher walk them to the building. The students had to consider the use of water bottles, the installation of water fountains outside, and what this would mean during the winter, safety concerns, and a host of other aspects.

In the fourth and fifth stages, students Design a Project and Implement the Action Plan. During these phases, students researched possible solutions and elaborated an action plan. This required analyzing different aspects of the issue and translating this into a concrete problem. Students had a chance to carry out what they have planned gathering resources.

In the final stage, coaches organize opportunities for Reflection, Communication, and Celebration. Within cycles of organizing, having the opportunity to reflect and actualize public accountability for the work is crucial. How do we evaluate the work, recognizing what was successful both in terms of the project but as importantly the processes? These moments for sharing the outcomes became powerful opportunities to bring in families but also created important sources of pressure to make sure students could share and use their voices to communicate their individual and collective successes. With little time, these presentations were often generated by coaches—whether a short movie or a scripted performance.

Walking Through an Example: Getting a Playground with Fourth Graders

After building relationships and agreements for their team, the fourth graders had to identify and think about possible projects. Through several iterations of walking around the school, drawing or writing ideas, the students expressed concern for the limited number of swings and play space particularly for the third through fifth graders. At the time, the school had two playgrounds with each playground being dedicated to the younger or older students. Students felt they had to wait in line for a long time and usually there were kids who would not get to swing.

Unlike most of the projects and coaches, this fourth-grade group was able to continue with their same coach for a year and had the support of the classroom teacher. Through the research with their coaches, they found out the district had closed one of the smaller schools and some of the students knew there was a playground there. The students invited the Assistant Superintendent of Operations to their afterschool class. With their coach, they had prepared for this meeting generating questions. The assistant superintendent went into all kinds of details about what the district looks for and how they pay for playgrounds. The team was interested in seeing if the district could move the playground from one of the elementary schools the district had closed. The assistant superintendent explained that trying to uproot the playground set for one school would probably end up breaking parts of the playground, making it more expensive and less safe to move. After the assistant superintendent had explained why he could not bring the playground from a school that would be closed and offered to match any fundraising the team did, one of the girls asked, "So is that a yes or a no on the playground?" While the answer was still "No," the students sought to push for a creative solution and were not concerned with raising questions.

The students were so disappointed, but the district was looking to upgrade playgrounds for several of the schools. The fourth graders organized a petition among their peers and wrote a letter to the principal and requested a new playground. With this, the team moved into a new phase of researching what kind of playgrounds would be good for the school. They learned that many new playgrounds did not actually have swings because these were deemed dangerous, and they learned about different surfaces. The students gathered input from peers showing them a couple examples they had selected from different catalogues. During this, each of the fourth graders had to provide explanations and share what they had learned.

Public Achievement has many examples of students developing projects around playgrounds, and in some ways, this is the most quintessential example of public work. Grasping self-interest, students come to embrace their life worlds and the recognition of the markers of social life and childhood represented by playgrounds. Rather than doing for others, students come to perceive the skill sets needed to advocate for improvements in their own communities.

Lessons Learned

At both school sites, our goal was to integrate Public Achievement into the curriculum teachers used to create new ways to engage in both curricular and pedagogical remaking. But in both cases, we experienced challenges in moving from the afterschool program to a deeply woven democratic experience in the classroom. In this next section, I point to our successes and challenges, contexts that supported or hindered the work, and the questions I still continue to grapple with in doing this work.

In my experience, the first school was positioned as a Community School both literally and figuratively at the center of the neighborhood. The principal was committed to developing the next generation of leaders and recognized the responsibility the school had in this process. Teachers often became burnout by all the changes and requests and what often started as voluntary and willing participants often shifted to teachers who grew resentful of the mandates. The afterschool program was not often fully staffed as funding cycles started to decrease in later years of the grant. This often meant that our first year college students with no or limited teaching experiences with their mentors often took on the job of staffing the program rather than supporting the program. This often led to coaches working in survival mode. In conversations with the PA supervisors, PA struggled because regular leadership meetings often failed to materialize with school leaders as a way to address these challenges.

At Transition School, we had a strong ally leading the afterschool program. She had been a long-time teacher at the school, was appreciated by families, and was committed to the Public Achievement program after attending many of the trainings with the Community School faculty. When she reapplied for the 21st Century Grant to fund the afterschool reading and math intervention programs, she would actually write in Public Achievement to highlight civic engagement. With experienced educators, stable groups with regular attendance of about 12–15 students, and somewhat clear expectations about where PA fit in, we had a ripe environment in which to integrate the program into the daily lives of classrooms.

But alas, this was not be the case. We adapted each year to trying to make PA fit more easily into the work of teachers. While the coaches came in one day a week, the teachers were organized around teaching reading or math four days a week, thus heavily impacting our ability to transform the space. We had coaches (few who would actually be pursuing teaching as a career) creating lesson plans trying to align with what teachers did the other days of the week when they focused on reading and math. We spent more time in the First Year Seminar learning how to lesson plan. The more we adapted to fit in to the structure, the more the expectations grew that we were doing what teachers were doing.

With teaching assistants and colleagues, we discussed how practical the course should be. How much should we theorize democratic principles and public work? How much should we prepare coaches to apprehend the realities of teaching and classroom management? How much time should we spend crafting stories about why we do the work we do and training students around the art of one-on-ones when these conversations would look so different in the context of their work with elementary school students?

In addition, we struggled constantly with the idea of continuity. Each semester we started anew with 15–25 first year students who would try to internalize a crash course around democracy and community organizing in 16 weeks with about 7–9 weeks in the elementary school classroom. Each of these teams would work to build relationships, conduct team-building, identify interests and possible projects, carry out the action plan, celebrate and reflect at the end of the semester. And we would start all over the following semester. How could we build and sustain a project over semesters and years in ways that would make the project more meaningful?

We deliberated on where we should spend most of our time while we were at the school. Should we go into classrooms and work with coaches? Should we work to support teachers? Should we identify student leaders in each of the teams so the continuity came from K-5 students who showed the most promise? Should we organize ourselves around the projects and make sure that every team had documentation of how they arrived at their issue and project and what conversations and decisions had led them to where they were? This way we would not have to worry about carrying out all six stages each semester.

Conclusion

Public work is a powerful motif that embraces the broader politics of teaching in this day and age. In many ways, public work allows teachers to avoid the partisan divides because it encourages the need to co-create tangible and material goods. While Public Achievement would probably allow for more politicized conversations, it is not necessarily grounded in a politics of contestation. Its greatest strength is the ability to allow everyday citizens, and in this case, young folks, the ability to envision a politics of what we can build together.

Public Achievement is a powerful program and recognizing the importance of being able to generate meaningful projects requires either more time or more input from the coaches and teachers. Our projects and our energy were most grounded when they went beyond the four walls of their classroom to encompass public skills and public actions—similar to the experiences with parents. While there are no easy answers and context matters, we need to start PA with teachers in classrooms committed to the idea of public work.

REFERENCES

Boyte, H. C. (2008). *The citizen solution: How you can make a difference.* Minnesota Historical Society Press.
Boyte, H. C. (2004). *Everyday politics: Reconnecting citizens and public life.* University of Pennsylvania Press.
Harris, A., Wyn, J., & Younes, S. (2010). Beyond apathetic or activist youth. *Nordic Journal of Youth Research, 18*(1), 9–32.
Kari, N. (2007). Public work: A practical theory. In N. Kari & N. Skelton (Eds.), *Voices of hope: The story of the Jane Addams School for Democracy* (pp. 24–38). Charles F. Kettering Foundation.
Noguera, P. (2003). *City schools and the American Dream: Reclaiming the promise of public education.* Teachers College Press.
Public Achievement. (n.d.). Inside Augsburg. Retrieved September 6, 2021, from https://sites.augsburg.edu/publicachievement/
The Six Stages of Public Achievement. (n.d.). Inside Augsburg. Retrieved September 6, 2021, from https://sites.augsburg.edu/publicachievement/teachers/six-stages-intro/

CHAPTER 6

The Power of Teacher Education

Abstract In this chapter, I focus on the ways in which teacher education can be more expansive to provide opportunities for civic engagement. Drawing on the history of the 1964 Freedom Schools and the concept of free spaces, I provide three examples of how I have worked to carve out spaces for civic engagement for teacher candidates. I consider the ways in which remaking of spaces can be intentionally situated in teacher education programs.

Keywords Teacher education • Civic engagement • 1964 Mississippi Freedom Schools • Free spaces • Social justice unionism

Opening Vignette

A teacher candidate raises the question during an education foundations course about the value of practicum. He says, "I'm not really sure what I'm supposed to be learning in practicum. I work with kindergarten students in small groups on their feelings journals or whatever else I'm assigned to do, but I'm not sure what to do." I ask more about the feelings journal, and he shares how the teacher uses the feelings journals to gauge how kids are doing before they start class by drawing what they are feeling and attaching a particular emotion. Part of a focus on socio-emotional learning, this activity helps teachers gauge where children may be on any particular day. On that particular day, he had helped the student express an emotion that was not on the chart. To address this, I suggest, "Maybe your role is to expand the range of emotions students can feel. And you certainly did that."

But taking a moment to consider the deeper implications of the question, I ask students to consider the following: "What if you are not there to learn how to teach but rather to learn to open up spaces to really come to understand who students are?" Since the student said he would try this, the next class I follow up with the student and ask, "How did it go?" Thoughtfully, he responds, "I really tried to follow up with a student on what he was drawing so I could come to understand him." The student had said, "I drew a picture of me holding a gun because I'm going to kill the other boy because he does not want to be my friend." This engagement provokes a recognition about the deep and complex worlds children inhabit and also awakens the need to enter the moral conversation about democracy. I ask, "What did you do?"

The teacher candidate was not sure what to do so we discussed a range of possibilities. "Did you talk with the student about how hard it was to be told we are no longer friends? Has that ever happened to you?" "What does it mean for kindergartners to talk about friendship?" "Did you share the incident with the teacher? Maybe the teacher has additional information about the student?" "Could you reach out to a counselor?"

As we thought about these issues in this class, the responses about what to do surprised me. While some teacher candidates thought it was important to follow up with the child to understand the situation better, others felt it was important to report the incident to administration. In some cases, teacher candidates felt it was necessary to call the police or establish whether the child or family had guns at home.

INTRODUCTION

Teacher education has often been situated within a place of certainty—best practices, effective teaching, recipes, and standardization (Cochran-Smith, 2004; Shuck & Buchanan, 2012). Teacher education is often conceptualized within a technocratic/rational approach that values methods (Chilcoat & Ligon, 1998). As Bransford et al. (2005) have highlighted, effective teachers need to articulate knowledge, skills, and commitments. How do we help teacher candidates deepen their commitments in ways that allow them to embrace a sense of uncertainty?

As the opening scenario above reflects, teacher education can and should invite teacher candidates to consider the complex life worlds of youth, the diverse needs and histories of families, and the uncertainty and ambiguity that make possible the humanizing potential of educational spaces. What would it mean to develop what Bartolome (1994) has termed ideological clarity? She describes this as "the process by which individuals struggle to identify and compare their own explanations for the existing socioeconomic and political hierarchy with those propagated by the dominant society" (p. xix). In this scenario, teacher candidates have to grapple with the moral meaning of democracy. What rights do children and adults have? How are those rights enacted?

Expanding our roles from teacher candidates to citizen teachers would require a deeper engagement with the communities in which we serve and learning how to make and remake educational spaces to rebuild society in ways that are more just and equitable (Counts, 1932). In Educational Foundations classes for teacher candidates, I ask students to map out the schools and communities in which they carry out their practicums to understand how their own biases and experiences may shape the way they construct their understandings. What does it mean to gather the stories and recognize the particular strengths and needs of a community? How do we come to understand the multiple stories that may exist in a community and how might we honor the experiences of folks that live in a particular community?

In this chapter, I provide some background on civic engagement and the 1964 Freedom Schools and consider how these ideas may inform our engagement as educators. Turning to the concept of free spaces, I underscore the ways in which citizen teachers can acquire the skills to produce spaces that are more equitable and more sustaining of justice. I then provide two examples of extracurricular spaces—Student Involvement Days (SIDs) and our Aspiring Educators union chapter. I end with Lessons Learned as a way to reflect on this journey.

Civic Engagement

Universities have listened to the clarion call of civic engagement. Through service-learning or the creation of civic service institutes, universities have tried to have more direct engagements with the communities to reduce town and gown issues—the disconnect that exists between universities and the communities in which they exist. Universities can and should provide resources and material supports for the communities in which they reside. Longo (2007) defines civic engagement

> as *public work* (projects creating things of public value); *community involvement* (membership in community groups and community service); *community organizing* (canvassing, protesting, and building power relations); *civic knowledge* (awareness of government processes and following public affairs); *conventional political action* (voting, campaign work, and advocacy for legislation); and *public dialogue* (deliberative conversations on public issues) (p. 14).

Bringing together public work with these other elements allows a cross-fertilization of ideas that promotes intentional forms of interaction that move beyond both volunteering and service-learning approaches.

While these foci around civic engagement have grown in universities, there are still important questions around how to engage civically in ways that disrupt the often one-sided approach where students take from the community without necessarily giving anything back. Similar to the experiments with settlement houses like Hull House in Chicago, civic engagement needs to be envisioned more expansively to create more bridges between and across formal and informal learning. As Longo (2007) has remarked, "A more expansive way of thinking about education for democracy means we must think *comprehensively, relationally, and publicly*" (p. 9). How can college students bring to bear their understandings of the theoretical engagements in classrooms while listening and learning from community members with whom they serve? How can we articulate important dimensions of civic work?

In colleges of education, fieldwork in the form of practicum and student teaching is often construed as civic engagement, but these engagements often lack what Longo described above. Teacher preparation programs generally focus more on preparing teachers for the classroom with little concern or ability to engage teacher candidates within the larger institutional or community structures. Partnerships can be lopsided and often power is not explicitly acknowledged. At best, teacher candidates work with mentor teachers who provide both freedom and guidance to experience teaching while acknowledging the parameters of teaching and learning in more holistic ways. At worst, teacher candidates have little sense of purpose and are provided few opportunities to understand classroom and school communities as "embryonic" communities (Dewey, 1991, p. 18).

1964 MISSISSIPPI FREEDOM SCHOOLS

In 1964, the Mississippi Freedom Summer Project organized by the Council of Federated Organizations (COFO), an umbrella organization for the Student Nonviolent Coordinating Council (SNCC) and other organizations, brought together African American activists and white students from northern universities to organize Freedom Schools, community centers, and voter registration drives (Emery et al., 2008). These efforts were intended to focus the country's attention on the conditions in Mississippi. Bob Moses and Charles Cobb, both members of the Student Nonviolent Coordinating Committee (SNCC), proposed the establishment of Freedom Schools in Mississippi. Recognizing the unequal opportunities available to African American youth in Mississippi public schools, Freedom Schools sought to identify and mobilize youth leaders while addressing the substandard education through academic and remedial education, leadership training, and a culturally relevant curriculum that connected young people to the Civil Rights Movement.

In this attempt to model education in the broadest sense of the word, Freedom Schools existed outside of the dominant structures while seeking to develop citizens who understood and could respond to the oppressive contexts of Mississippi schools. This required embracing a framework and curriculum that would adapt easily to the conditions and the participants. In thinking through this idea of curricular adaptation, volunteers were "told to discard it and to create, on the spot if necessary, activities and questions that responded to the needs of the students in front of them. The curriculum's central premise, the importance of questioning, challenged the concept of a written curriculum" (Emery et al., n.d.). Central to this was valuing the questions and experiences of participants above all else and generating spaces that taught leadership.

COMMUNITY ORGANIZING CONCEPT: FREE SPACES

In an effort to recognize the possibilities to developing leadership capacities, I was envisioning teacher education outside of the constraints of the formal curriculum. In many ways, classrooms were spaces for the identification of talented individuals with a vision and commitment to social justice. Fundamental to all of these engagements outside of teacher education was the creation of free spaces—spaces where teacher candidates could envision themselves as actively involved in social justice engagements. In describing free spaces, Evans and Boyte (1986/1992) wrote:

Environments in which people are able to learn a new self-respect, a deeper and more assertive group identity, public skills, and values of cooperation and civic virtue. Put simply, free spaces are settings between private lives and large-scale institutions where ordinary citizens can act with dignity, independence, and vision (p. 17).

In the different examples below, we sought to generate more justice-oriented spaces by both recruiting teacher candidates with lived experiences grounded in understanding social justice or creating the conditions for teacher candidates to develop capacities to imagine anew. Building on the ideas from Public Achievement in Chap. 5, these spaces were intended to allow for and reflect democratic deliberation.

In envisioning these spaces, I recognized the prevalence of dominant ideologies that shaped the spaces I was in—the College of Education at a public university, charter school, and the National Education Association (NEA) Aspiring Educators student union (AE student union). In the College of Education teacher education program, technocratic rationalities and the reproduction of strategies were strongly sedimented into the foundations. Teacher candidates often expressed appreciation for their fieldwork experiences in practicum on showing them how to teach and address "real world issues" and the disconnect between courses that were not directly tied to what they saw in the classroom. For each of these spaces, our work consisted of creating spaces outside of the dominant understandings of what these spaces were.

STUDENT INVOLVEMENT DAYS: PUTTING FREEDOM SCHOOL PRINCIPLES INTO PRACTICE

My work at the Mountain English Spanish Academy (M.E.S.A.), a small charter middle school housed in Community School, provided me with an important community space to test out ideas. In 2008, the district evicted the charter school from its location, and we moved to a small strip mall storefront that had previously been a dance studio and church respectively (Wood, 2020).The charter school board composed primarily of district school board members also moved to sever ties with the charter school. With these ties removed and the keys to the building, I had relative autonomy to organize several afterschool clubs and events.

Drawing explicitly on the Freedom Schools model, Students Involvement Days (SIDs) formulated an explicitly political and social justice-oriented curriculum to engage pre-service teachers in an alternative educational format. Organized one weekend a month, SIDs attempted to create a more rigorous and relevant curriculum for marginalized youth. Often challenging the rote memorization and drill and skill exercises found in urban school settings, SIDs encouraged participants to name their experiences and identify ways to challenge anti-immigrant and anti-youth legislation and practices. I was able to use the charter school space and operate outside of the formal constraints a large school district might impose when considering having middle school students spend the night in the school with university students and faculty.

For Student Involvement Day (SID), I was hoping to imagine how teacher candidates could be part of building spaces outside of the regular constraints of schools. In describing Student Involvement Day, I wrote:

> Student Involvement Days will focus more on creating political awareness and youth leadership in the Sunnyside community focusing on the work of the Freedom Schools... NAU students have the opportunity to test out ideas and bring in their expertise/passion in ways that are often not acknowledged by schools.

With a powerful team of university students who brought in a range of experiences, passions, and interests, we created a space where M.E.S.A. students and their families could be a part of the educational process. Youth (middle and elementary school students) would arrive to the school on Saturday morning for a line-up of different events around a range of themes and activities (e.g. poetry, welding, laying down beats and telling stories through hip hop). In the afternoon, families were invited to participate in a closing ceremony where young people shared their work—often skits, poetry, or other types of work. After this, only the middle school students and the university students and faculty would participate in evening conversations, movies, and spending the night at the school; these conversations and activities were both invigorating and exhausting, profound and humbling as teacher candidates etched out the very margins of what their limits could be—whether talking about friendship or sexual abuse, relationships or loss, identity and culture. These conversations stretched me to my core as I saw these young teacher candidates expanding the boundaries of what was possible but also wondering how they might fit in to the constraints of public school.

As I looked at agendas from our Student Involvement Days, questions that drove my thinking were: "1) How do youth start to name racism and sexism in ways that are empowering? 2) How can young people get engaged in making positive changes in their community?" One of the SIDs focused on homelessness. Having read that Flagstaff was one of the ten meanest cities in the country for the way in which it criminalized homeless folks, the idea was to generate a space to interrogate and respond to these policies. After reading and discussing the policy, students performed alternative versions of "The Three Little Pigs," paying attention to alternative understandings that shaped homelessness. Within the context of SID, one of our families who was experiencing homelessness spent the night at the school further underscoring the reality of this experience.

Role play became an important conduit for our work. As a result of concerns expressed by students around harassment and by parents around immigration, participants enacted several role plays to highlight knowledge of their rights. The scenarios included being stopped by the police while walking on the street, adults being stopped by the police for a traffic violation, and Immigration and Customs Enforcement (ICE) officers coming to a person's home. Participants expressed surprise by their reactions to authority often providing more information than necessary. Participants learned to respond to these scenarios by knowing what information to share and what authority law enforcement had or did not have.

The power of protest was reflected in the interactions young people saw in their communities. The deportation of 16 individuals had led to an impromptu protest in the community. SID participants came across this protest against ICE in their neighborhood. While none of their family members protested because of their fear, participants recognized the power of protest. All the photographs focused on the protest and highlighted how protest could mobilize people to act.

Arts were also a necessary component for imagining new possibilities. Using cameras, students documented the realities of their community and compared these to other communities. One participant took pictures of the area outside of the school, which was littered with broken glass and trash. On the other hand, her other set of pictures depicted the cleanliness of the parking lot. Her presentation alluded to the powerful disconnect between these two worlds and allowed for the beginning of a conversation around what she envisioned for her school.

This work would continue after the school closed with my now life partner and several other students and community members. We met at a local community center or the university where we tackled ways to recognize meaningful curricular and pedagogical experiences that reflected students' identities. With the banning of Ethnic Studies, specifically the Mexican American Studies Program in Tucson, AZ, this provided us with an important opportunity to acknowledge youth's experiences in schools. Elementary and middle school youth mapped out culturally embracing or threatening school spaces based on how they reflected their identities. In addition, youth watched a movie based on the 1969 Chicano Student Blowouts. Students then explored how they might raise these issues in school by identifying supportive teachers and modeling conversations around what clues and responses would allow youth to open up conversations with their teachers. After attending a youth conference in Tucson, youth came back to the local school district and spoke up at board meetings about the need for Ethnic Studies. In the second example, I highlight the work of union organizing.

Aspiring Educators Union Chapter: Social Justice Unionism

As I describe in Chap. 1, effective teacher union organizing has moved to consider the broader implications of equity in the communities in which educators serve. Grassroots organizing push for equity in #RedforEd and conversations about Bargaining for the Common Good highlight the importance of moving beyond traditional unionism and professional unionism. Within traditional unionism, members of the union often in a hierarchical fashion advocate for bread and butter issues for their members and other employees who would benefit from higher pay and better working conditions. Over the course of six years, we have formed an Aspiring Educators union chapter to support teacher candidates. NEA has sought to instill the importance of union membership before educators enter the field with the hopes of developing a stronger sense of union participation.

In our first years, my focus as the sole advisor was to push students to articulate clearly a commitment to social justice. Several student organizations existed in the College—Future Teachers Club (FTC) and Kappa Delta Pi (KDP)—that were popular for our students. FTC was the brainchild of one of my former colleague who created a space for students to love and be inspired by teaching and teachers. KDP was an honor society built on the pillars of Knowledge, Duty, and Power; this group invited teacher candidates to join depending on their Grade Point Average (GPA). These two organizations had similar structures—social organizations that required attendance and participation in community service in ways that advocated volunteerism rather than public work. In the absence of spaces that promoted social justice and broad-based organizing, the Aspiring Educators union chapter provided me with a breath of fresh air bringing in more critical perspectives. Organizing teach-ins around different history or heritage months, these events were open to the general public and required outreach to groups or faculty across campus or required executive board members to interface with NEA.

While the Aspiring Educators union chapter has shifted with the election of different executive boards, this chapter has developed a strong sense of commitment around its four pillars—Teacher Quality, Community Engagement, Political Action, and Social Justice. Throughout the years, the strongest focus has been on generating critical social justice topics (e.g. LGBTQ seminars to address No Promo Homo laws, School to Prison Pipeline, Climate Change, the War on Critical Race Theory) and some political action work around #RedforEd or increased funding for schools. Teacher candidates have been engaged in writing grants; communicating with national, state, and local union officials; organizing events; and developing recruitment strategies with extensive support from NEA and the Arizona Education Association (AEA). We have had members attend the NEA Representative Assembly to understand how NEA prioritizes issues important to its membership.

One year, our union chapter heard from several teacher candidates that their practicum placements left much to be desired—grading, busy work, making copies, and limited interactions with students were at the crux of these concerns. With some prompting from advisors, the executive board decided to create a survey for teacher candidates in their practicum placements. When the administration got wind of this, they created several roadblocks and tried to stop the survey. Several of our executive board members learned to negotiate spaces with the administration with the support of advisors. Eventually, the administration agreed to the survey but also appropriated it for its own purposes.

As the teacher candidates have developed exemplary programming, other student organizations, particularly Educators Rising, have started to generate similar conversations through some cross-fertilization of advisors. With these spaces now geared toward social justice, I wanted us to gravitate back to union organizing. I had grown concerned with the dangers of complacency, the rigid scheduling of weekly meetings (often mapped out months in advance), and the lack of focus on traditional union organizing.

Union Stewardship

During the last executive boards 2021–2022, two different teacher candidates raised concerns about interactions with faculty. Using these concerns, I asked executive board members if they would be willing to accompany one of their peers to meetings with the faculty and academic chair of the department to serve as witnesses or if they felt comfortable as union representatives. I also talked with Jeff, our NEA Aspiring Educators Organizer, about what support we would have. Jeff immediately offered to hear the teacher candidates' grievances and/or attend the meetings as needed. He also clarified that we do have access to liability insurance. I brought this information to the board with the hopes they would discuss and decide on whether they wanted to serve as teacher candidate advocates in similar ways that union building reps would represent educators.

In the Fall of 2021 with two seniors getting ready for student teaching as co-presidents and only two months left, timing was an issue. How would we get the last board to bring this to the executive board and the membership for discussion and a vote? The board was not used to running meetings that would require votes or actions. Finding myself in the position of trying to add this to our agenda and being continuously deflected without a real conversation, we were not able to institute serving as union stewards to defend the rights of our student members. As the new board took over, I encountered the same issues with the board—a president student teaching and getting ready to graduate who kept suggesting the new board could tackle all these questions.

Changing the Structure

As we began with a new board for Fall 2022, we had to move quickly with our team of advisors and our student union to ensure conditions would be put in place to make sure the new board would not reproduce the model from the last two boards—powerful weekly conversations mapped out months in advance with little opportunity to react and respond to changing conditions for teachers. During the ad hoc executive board meetings,

I, along with my co-advisors, had tried to raise the issue of a different structure of meetings to allow for more action-oriented meetings, ensuring only members had the right to vote, and running meetings with Robert's Rules of Order. These issues usually got pushed to the end of the meeting, leaving little time for discussion. We collectively met as advisors to clarify and solidify our expectations for the next elections and the next board. When we discussed having only paying members vote, the president said all people running for the executive board know they have to pay dues to be on the board. I replied, "People should not pay to be on the board. They should pay because they believe in the union." The conversation ended with the president making the final decision that anyone at the meeting could vote.

To ensure a more democratic process moving forward, advisors generated a list of criteria to be put in place including only members could vote, only teacher candidates who would be eligible for a one-year term (could not be student teaching with a caveat), and we eliminated most of the co-positions that had been created by the past board to ensure every person running got a position and created new positions that would ensure attention to the transitions we were trying to make—a Recruitment Chair, a Member Chair, a National Campaign Coordinator, a Local Union Liaison, and a Parliamentarian along with the more traditional roles. We sent off a couple of messages a few days before the election expecting some pushback. With one of the other advisors working with the president who would not be running for a position, we pushed through some necessary changes and created an important dialogue in a group chat about what these changes meant. While not entirely democratic, the conversation prompted incredible engagement from current executive board members making the constitution, bylaws, and position descriptions a necessary conversation to tackle.

Transitioning Toward Social Justice Unionism

In the summer and fall of 2022, I hope the university union will be able to see the critical need to move to a kind of social justice unionizing (Peterson, 2021). In this vision, I hope we will be able to practice solidarity with our union colleagues standing side by side in the fight to certify the local union while building deep and meaningful ties with educators in the broader struggles in our community. I hope we will have robust commitments to social justice embodied through critical engagements with topics and ideas existing within the nexus of both teacher practice and aspiring educators' beliefs—the reality of the world as it is embodied in teachers on the front lines and the vision and passion enshrined in the hopes of our teacher candidates. I have high hopes that we be able to build a national campaign to ensure greater teacher professionalism and autonomy pushing against new mandates, which restrict the field in which educators work and imagine new possibilities.

Lessons Learned

In Chap. 5, I highlighted how Public Achievement needed to be embedded and embodied in the daily work of teachers. Should this be any different in the work of teacher educators and teacher candidates in a College of Education? All this work I described existed outside of formal curricular channels.

In these free spaces (Evans & Boyte, 1986/1992) where we have carved out a vision that runs counter to the understandings of what teachers do, we have encountered resistance from colleagues, from peers, and from college leadership. In order to resist these challenges, these practices and understandings have to be part of the formal teacher education curriculum and have to be modelled in their practicum and student teaching placements. In conversations with former students who have been part of this work, I wonder how they translate this work as they become teachers. Without ongoing conversations and support, I have seen the majority revert back to not using or applying these ideas.

Conclusion

Many years ago when I was involved with M.E.S.A., the small charter school, I would often encourage teacher candidates to go engage with students at the school. In one particular instance, two young white women came back after their first time at the school and said, "Gerald, we are not going back." I asked why. The teacher candidates expressed fear being in the school. Many of the students were probably physically larger than the teacher candidates, and they were all Students of Color. I asked them, "What did you do while you were there?" After some prompting, one of the women said, "We stood against the back wall the whole time we were there because we were so scared." I told the two young women, "Do me a favor. Go back one more time and get to know one of the middle school students. Come back and tell me their story. If you don't want to go back after that, no worries." A couple days later, the two women came back and before I could ask them anything, they started blurting out with excitement the stories they had learned from the students. Both women ended up going back regularly to the school.

As I recall this story, I am reminded of Bryan Stevenson's (2015) conversation regarding prison inmates around proximity and the need to get close to those who are most marginalized in order to begin to understand our own humanity. Civic engagement allows us to become proximate to those whose stories we cannot understand until we cross literal and figurative borders. It provides us with opportunities to learn from and with members of the community while allowing us to envision more robust spaces deeply embedded in communities. By listening to members of our community with different lived experiences than our own, we come to know the partiality of our own knowing and the limits of our hopes and fears. By reconceptualizing teacher education in ways more aligned with civic engagement, we can find alternative ways to feel a sense of connectedness that is rooted in genuine knowledge of self and others.

References

Bartolome, L. I. (1994). *Ideologies in education: Unmasking the trap of teacher neutrality.* Peter Lang.

Bransford, J., Darling-Hammond, L., & LePage, P. (2005). Introduction. In L. Darling-Hammond & J. Bransford (Eds.), *Preparing teachers for a changing world: What teachers should learn and be able to do* (pp. 1–39). Jossey-Bass.

Chilcoat, G. W., & Ligon, J. A. (1998). "We talk here. This is a school for talking.": Participatory democracy from the classroom out into the community: How discussion was used in the Mississippi Freedom Schools. *Curriculum Inquiry, 28*(2), 165–193.

Cochran-Smith, M. (2004). Editorial: The problem of teacher education. *Journal of Teacher Education, 55*(4), 295–299. https://doi.org/10.1177/0022487104268057

Counts, G. S. (1932). *Dare the schools build a new social order?* Pref by W. J. Urban. Southern Illinois University Press.

Dewey, J. (1991). *The school and society and the child and the curriculum.* Centennial Publication. Intro. by P.W. Jackson. University of Chicago Press.

Emery, K., Reid Gold, L., & Braselmann, S. (2008). *Lessons from Freedom Summer: Ordinary people building extraordinary movements.* Common Courage Press.

Emery, K., Braselmann, S., & Reid Gold, L. (n.d.). *Mississippi Freedom School Curriculum*. Education and Democracy. Retrieved June 6, 2022, from http://www.educationanddemocracy.org/ED_FSC.html

Evans, S., & Boyte, H. C. (1986/1992). *Free spaces: The sources of democratic change in America*. The University of Chicago Press.

Longo, N. V. (2007). *Why community matters: Connecting education with civic life*. State University of New York.

Peterson, B. (2021). A revitalized teacher union movement: Reflections from the field. In M. Charney, J. Hagopian, & B. Peterson (Eds.), *Teacher unions and social justice: Organizing for the schools and communities we deserve* (pp. 237–247). A Rethinking Schools Publication.

Shuck, S., & Buchanan, J. (2012). Dead certainty: The case for doubt in teacher education. *Australian Journal of Teacher Education, 37*(8), 1–11.

Stevenson, B. (2015). *Just mercy: A story of justice and redemption* (Reprint ed.). One World.

Wood, G. (2020). Troubling sanctuary: Excavating the moral and educational wreckage of the charter school movement. *International Journal of Educational Policies, 13*(2), 111–143.

CHAPTER 7

Conclusion

Abstract The conclusion provides an account of how the work at Transition School ended and invites readers to consider how they may get started in the work. This chapter also suggests how this work might be in the self-interest of teachers.

Keywords Teacher authority • Classrooms as movement-building spaces • Moral meaning of democracy • Humanization • Solidarity

OPENING VIGNETTE

During the third year of organizing in the school, I was called in to the principal's office. I had not been called to the principal's office since second grade when I went along with some friends to hide on the buses before it was time to go home. I expected this to be a dressing down by the principal who had raised her concern about segregating parents or had walked away defensively from some of the meetings. Or was it possibly about a parent like Selena who threatened the principal's authority to her core?

So when I was called into a meeting with Kelly, the principal, and the afterschool coordinator, I was caught off guard particularly when I found out Kelly had called the meeting. Kelly, one of the teachers, had been central to our organizing work at Transition School. She had initiated the

© The Author(s), under exclusive license to Springer Nature Switzerland AG 2022
G. K. Wood, *Citizen Teachers and the Quest for a Democratic Society*, https://doi.org/10.1007/978-3-031-15464-5_7

neighborhood walks and expressed strong feelings about how she was treated by parents during parent pickup. She was a phenomenal educator whom I believed understood the need to connect to the communities in which we served. Kelly's main concern focused on the use of agitation during individual meetings. I responded to this by saying, "Agitation is one of the many things we do in organizing to understand parents and to identify their motivations to act."

As we continued talking, the conversation seemed hopeless. Each explanation was met with the suggestion that I should continue doing what I was doing but maybe not agitate parents. As I addressed the role that agitation played, she would bring up another concern as she attempted to dismantle one thing after another. I suggested each of these pieces for individual meetings was fundamental to the process of building relationships with parents and to identifying leaders. Furthermore, I argued this model operated cohesively. Similar to what the school was trying to do with Success for All in terms of implementing the whole model, I countered with the question, "What if I suggested that you should not have the Parent and Family Involvement Team?" Both the principal and the teacher jumped in quickly to explain you could not carry out Success for All without all the pieces. I agreed the same was true for organizing; all pieces were necessary.

By the time we finished, the principal and teacher had boiled down their request to, "Could you just call parents to invite them to meetings?" Deeply offended and knowing that the power of organizing came from these deep relationships, I answered, "I cannot invite parents I do not know. You want me to be like a secretary?" After much deliberation, I decided to leave. I was sad to leave the parents and educators whom I had come to know and respect.

Introduction

While I do not know for sure what precipitated Kelly's decision to call the meeting, I can venture some educated guesses. Kelly had also been one of the teachers who had led the discussion of the color of shirts children could wear for Valentine's Day during the Parent and Family Involvement Team at the expense of hearing parents' concerns regarding attendance and parent-teacher conferences. We can be fearful when we are not in control, and parent organizing without teachers in the mix gives rise to important fears about authority. My mentor and friend, Dr. Guy Senese, has spoken to the importance of teacher authority and the centrality of moral claims to democracy (Mizikaci & Senese, 2017). How could we ground our authority not solely in our training as professionals but also in our ability to serve as go-betweens of our professional realm of expertise and the communities we serve?

Teacher Identities as Citizen Teachers

As I have argued, citizen teachers need to reconceptualize themselves as citizens first. Only by doing so can educators start to move outside the realm of their partial understandings that may frame parents and students through a deficit lens. In our own profession, we have been trained to evaluate students and this comes with judgments about parents—about their capacity to parent, about their willingness or ability to participate in what school determines as important, and about the narratives parents may be generating for their children. Without breaking out of our institutional roles, we will not have the capacity to ask questions that humanize or exist outside of the direct realm of our interactions with families.

To open ourselves up to listen to how parents bring in a wealth of knowledge from their communities allows us to see parents as people first. Individual meetings allow us to probe the depth of human experience. Whether talking about politics, faith, parenting, trials and tribulations, motivations and actions, and most importantly values, we can no longer see parents as only existing in relationship to their children but as citizens with larger commitments. Our relationships will not be dictated by institutional roles that have traditionally been layered in hierarchies but rather driven by the belief in the fundamental and collective responsibilities we have as citizens—in the broadest sense conveyed in this book through this idea of everyday politics and public work.

Border Crossings and the Mobilizations of Broader Collective Interests

If spaces are products of social relationships that are mediated by power, citizen teachers must be able to cross and bridge institutional and community borders. This would allow new configurations of relationships and alter the undemocratic spaces that often exist in schools. As I have documented, teachers can and must envision their classrooms as movement-building spaces (Anyon, 2014). Having young people to bring in their lives and to make their lives central to the curriculum allows a new engagement with teaching that is grounded in the lives of communities.

Citizen teachers must recognize how privilege allows for or hinders their ability to work with communities in ways that allow for genuine dialogue. Only when we acknowledge the struggles our families face will we be able to speak to our own humanity—teacher burnout, moonlighting trying to make ends meet, staying late at school to care for our students knowing our own children may not have parents at home, and facing the laws that require us to disregard both our training and our values as human beings. To enter into these humanizing dialogues with families, teachers must acknowledge our own self-interest to improve working conditions and to ensure treatment as professionals.

Getting Started

We must begin with the humility as educators that we do not and cannot have all the answers. If this is the case, how can we listen to parents to stretch our understandings of the hopes and fears that would allow us to be more grounded in democratic traditions?

To start, let's work to create spaces for parents to be co-creators of democratic spaces. Start small. Let's build meaningful relationships with a small number of parents who may bring in different lived experiences and knowledges than our own to understand the richness and complexities that shape families and communities. Ask school leaders to create spaces for dialogue between educators and parents.

Let families see you present in their neighborhoods. Attend events in the community. Ask questions to learn. Create genuine understandings of the strengths and needs of the communities you serve. Conduct neighborhood walks with other educators and parents to hear about the traditions, experiences, and challenges that families embrace and encounter. Reach out and host meetings in different neighborhoods to center relationships in communities rather than in the school. These signals are important to community members who have experienced schooling as often violent or oppressive.

Pay attention to the messages you send to communities. Does your marquis signal collaboration and allyship? Is your communication with families unidirectional or does it invite families to share concerns about the school or community? Do you have spaces that allow families to share their questions, experiences, and hopes rather than just enact the rituals expected by the school? Is your school cognizant of the issues facing the community and does your school host events to address these issues? Does your school have staff that reflect the communities you serve?

Identify community organizations that have trained organizers in your community. Develop partnerships that allow your school to build the capacity to organize. Consider what it would mean to build power recognizing the expertise and needs of all community members to further a collective agenda.

Conclusion

Can we ask educators to do more? I believe we must, but this work can only be sustained and meaningful when it is carefully orchestrated through a much broader lens of public accountability. Teachers already do so much to support children and families individually, but addressing each of these as individual needs expends incredible time and energy. By combining these struggles and weaving these with specific challenges schools face, citizen teachers can begin to imagine a much wider set of concerns.

Teachers can and must demand the impossible—to be treated as professionals who command the respect of families, communities, and politicians. However, to engage as citizen teachers, teachers must lead in the "formation of public opinion" by brokering an enlarged scope of responsibility that is generated from the proximity, concern, and power educators can mobilize when listening to communities (Dewey, 1913, p. 38).

Why should teachers listen to parents and families? Because parents and families provide us with the capacity to imagine a world that is more just and more sustainable. When parents become our allies, they will also stand side by side to advocate with us and for us. By expanding the range of issues, we will develop the ability to organize across multiple issues in ways that expand our moral authority as educators but more importantly our democratic claims as citizens.

To create more just schools, citizen teachers can and must be border crossers that acknowledge the collective struggles facing communities and the solutions identified by and with community members. Through coalition-building, citizen teachers building power to recognize the importance of teacher professionalism, the claims to robust forms of democratic engagement, and networks of solidarity that will allow teachers to be valued because they are citizens first.

References

Anyon, J. (2014). *Radical possibilities: Public policy, urban education, and a new social movement* (2nd ed.). Routledge.

Dewey, J. (1913). Professional spirit among teachers. In D. J. Simpson, & S. F. Stack, Jr. (Eds.), 2010 *Teachers, leaders, and schools: Essays by John Dewey* (pp. 37–40). Southern Illinois University Press.

Mizikaci, F., & Senese, G. (2017). *A language of freedom and teacher's authority: Case comparisons from Turkey and the United States.* Lexington Books.

Index[1]

NUMBERS AND SYMBOLS
#RedforEd, 9–12, 93, 94

A
Accountability, 6, 26, 35, 40, 41, 44–45, 47, 50, 55, 56, 59–60, 66, 79, 105
Addams, Jane, 12
Allies, ix, 10, 49, 55, 81, 105
Altering spaces, 56
Anger (hot and cold), 63
Anyon, Jean, 2, 3, 13, 17, 55, 63, 104
Arizona, ix, xi, xvi, 1, 2, 6, 10, 11, 29
Aspiring Educators, 39, 59, 87, 90, 93–97

B
Black porters, 8
Border crossing, xi, 37–38, 51, 103–104
Border pedagogy, 37–38
Borders, xiii, 3, 14, 16, 18, 68, 98, 103, 105
Boyte, Harry, 13n1, 14, 73–75, 89, 97
Broad-based organizing, 94
Bullying, 53–55, 61, 67, 72, 78

C
Charter school, 1, 6, 7, 16, 26, 37, 90, 91, 97
Chicago, 4, 7–8, 10–12, 25, 26, 28, 62, 88
Citizen professionals, 14–15
Citizen teacher, xvii, 1–18, 21–31, 87, 103–105
Civic engagement, 73, 81, 87–88, 98
Class struggle, 7, 8
Co-creators, 3, 55, 58, 73, 74, 104
Collective, 7, 8, 10, 12–14, 16, 23, 56–58, 60, 62, 63, 79, 103–105

---

[1] Note: Page numbers followed by 'n' refer to notes.

© The Author(s), under exclusive license to Springer Nature Switzerland AG, part of Springer Nature 2022
G. K. Wood, *Citizen Teachers and the Quest for a Democratic Society*, https://doi.org/10.1007/978-3-031-15464-5

Common good (Bargaining for the Common Good (BGC)), 10
Community, vii–xii, xiiin2, xiv–xvii, 2, 3, 5, 7–10, 12–18, 21–29, 30n3, 31, 35, 37–42, 44–48, 50, 51, 55–59, 61, 62, 67, 72–77, 76n1, 80, 87–94, 96, 98, 102–105
Community cultural wealth, 37
Community organizing, 3, 7–8, 12, 13, 13n1, 16–18, 35, 38–43, 50, 55, 56, 58–62, 64, 73–75, 77, 82, 88–90
See also Organizing
Convergence, 3, 13, 35
Corporate reformers, 6
Counts, George, 9, 13, 87
COVID-19, 4, 27–28
See also Pandemic
Critical geographies of/in education, 27
Critical Race Theory, 5, 94
Cultural brokers (brokers), 27, 37
Curriculum, 4, 5, 22, 44, 51, 56, 57, 61, 64–65, 68, 76, 77, 80, 89, 91, 97, 104

D
Democratic professionalism, 14
Dewey, John, vii, viii, 4, 5, 9, 12, 14, 37, 88, 105
Divestment (public education), 4, 6–7

E
Education organizing, 7–9, 55–56
Everyday politics, 75, 103

F
"Factoryizing" education, 5
Freedom School (1964 Mississippi), 16, 87, 89
Free spaces, 87, 89–90, 97

G
Great Migration, 8

H
Haley, Margaret, 5, 8, 9, 13n1
Haymarket Square, 7
Historical trauma, 30n3
See also Intergenerational trauma
House meetings, 48, 53, 55, 60–61, 63, 64, 67
Humanizing, 15, 37, 87, 104

I
Immigration, 2, 16, 61, 92
Individual meetings (one-on-ones, relational meetings), 40–43, 46–47, 51, 60, 61, 66, 77, 81, 102, 103
Industrial Areas Foundation (IAF), 13, 16, 38, 41, 45, 61–64, 67
Intergenerational trauma, 30, 30n3, 43
Intermediaries, 14, 17

L
Labor movement, 9
Legislation, 6, 88, 91
LGBTQ+, 94
Lipsitz, George, 25, 27, 36, 56

M
Moral authority, 5, 105
Movement-building spaces, 17, 104

N
National Education Association (NEA), 9, 39, 59, 90, 93–95
Northern Arizona Interfaith Council (NAIC), 16, 43, 44

O

Organizing, viii–x, xvi, 3, 4, 7, 8, 10–13, 17, 18, 30, 33–51, 54–57, 59–62, 67, 68, 71–82, 93–95, 101, 102

P

Pandemic, 4, 27
Parent engagement, 29, 43, 55, 57–59
Parent involvement, 30, 43, 55, 58–59, 64
Pedagogy, 5, 38
Place-making, 17, 21–31
Power, relational power, ix, xvi, 3, 6, 7, 9, 11–13, 15, 16, 23, 24, 27, 33–51, 53–68, 71–82, 85–98, 102, 103, 105
Professional spirit, 4, 5
Public Achievement (PA), 13n1, 17, 18, 71–82, 90, 97
Public work, 14, 17, 40, 41, 56, 60, 72–75, 80–82, 88, 94, 103
Pullman Strikes, 8

R

Racialized geographies, 17, 21–31
Racism, 92
Relationships, (public vs. private), 47

S

Schools, vii, xi, 1, 22–26, 33, 53, 71, 87, 101
School shootings (mass), 27, 28
Self-interest (genuine), 3
Settler colonialism, 25n1

Shirley, Dennis, 45, 55, 56, 58, 60, 64
Social centers, 12
Social justice, xiii, xx, 5, 89, 90, 93, 94, 96
Social justice unionism, 93–97
Sociological imagination, 15, 16
Space (production of space, spatial), 18, 22–28
Spatial imaginary
  Black, 55–57
  white, 35–37
Strikes, 7, 10, 11
Success for All, 30–31, 65, 102

T

Trust, 35, 50, 59, 60

U

Unions, ix, 6–12, 39, 59, 87, 90, 93–97
  See also National Education Association (NEA); Social justice unionism

V

Volunteering, 16, 56, 58, 88

W

Warren, Mark, 13, 39, 55, 58
White supremacy, 2, 5, 6, 18, 23, 25
Whiteness, xv, 16, 18, 35–37, 57
Women's work, 5
Working conditions (teachers), 3–5

Printed by Printforce, United Kingdom